Also by Lee Woodruff

*In an Instant: A Family's Journey of Love
and Healing* (with Bob Woodruff)

PERFECTLY IMPERFECT

To Angie —

Perfectly Imperfect

A Life in Progress

LEE WOODRUFF

Introduction by Bob Woodruff

RANDOM HOUSE TRADE PAPERBACKS · NEW YORK

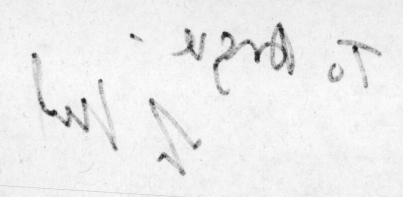

2010 Random House Trade Paperback Edition

Published in the United States by Random House Trade Paperbacks,
an imprint of The Random House Publishing Group,
a division of Random House, Inc., New York.

RANDOM HOUSE TRADE PAPERBACKS and colophon are
trademarks of Random House, Inc.

Originally published in hardcover in the United States by Random House,
an imprint of The Random House Publishing Group,
a division of Random House, Inc., in 2009.

LIBRARY OF CONGRESS CATALOGING-IN-PUBLICATION DATA
Woodruff, Lee.
Perfectly imperfect: a life in progress / Lee Woodruff.
p. cm.
ISBN 978-0-8129-7902-2
1. Woodruff, Lee. 2. Woodruff, Lee—Family.
3. Woodruff, Lee—Philosophy. 4. Woodruff, Bob.
5. Women—United States—Biography. 6. Journalists' spouses—
United States—Biography. 7. Family—United States. I. Title.
CT275.W6665A3 2009   973.931092—dc22   2008028842
[B]

Printed in the United States of America

www.atrandom.com

5 6 7 8 9

Book design by Dana Leigh Blanchette

To my children, who each taught me in various ways to slow down, to observe the little moments, to listen, and to laugh at myself.

And to Bob, for showing me that anything really is possible.

Contents

Introduction

Bob Woodruff

I feel incredibly fortunate to have met Lee more than two decades ago, and not just because we fell in love, got married, had wonderful children, and only really fight seriously once a year. (Okay—maybe twice a year, but once is always about money.) Reading this book highlighted the qualities I see when I'm with Lee in person: humor, honesty, poignancy, irreverence, reflection, and just plain warmth. She writes just the way she talks. Reading these chapters is like sitting on a porch where Lee is regaling a group of friends with some funny stories.

She can somehow move effortlessly between humor and sorrow, joy and pathos, almost as if she is not one person, but many. She has the uncanny ability to capture a moment and describe what others are feeling. It is her complexity and accessibility with which I fell in love. She probably could have been an actress or a comedian, a writer for television or of screenplays. Instead, she married me and set up house in various towns around the country and overseas as my career kept us on the move and our family grew. Being a mother was then, and still is, the heart of her life. But she always kept writing.

For many years, especially early on in my journalism career, Lee used her writing skills to pen magazine articles and corporate brochures, public relations materials and videos for businesses, "anything to pay the bills," as she would say in the lean days when my salary barely covered the rent. And when I finally earned a respectable wage, still, she kept writing. It was her catharsis, the thing she did for herself and a way to chronicle the small moments of family life, the funny and touching anecdotes that might otherwise be forgotten over the years.

For twenty-two years Lee has been making me laugh with her observations and her keen take on the world. And for all that time I've been encouraging her to write a book. So nothing could make me happier than to write an introduction for her first solo effort.

When we, as a team, wrote our book *In an Instant,* I concentrated on facts and memories while she poured out feelings and emotion; this is the difference between our two styles. During my injury and recovery I was amazed, watching my wife, at how she was able to keep so many things together—the children's needs and schedules, while managing their fears and concerns. Lee is quick to point out on these pages that multitasking isn't my strong suit, and I've looked on with awe as Lee has juggled her career, motherhood, friendships, and family responsibilities throughout our entire marriage.

Now, with *Perfectly Imperfect,* she has created a volume of stories about those collective experiences. Each chapter contains commonalities, the observances that many women, and even men, will be able to relate to as they see themselves on the pages.

I am honored to share my life and my wife with you in this way. And may her journey enrich your own world in some small way.

PERFECTLY IMPERFECT

Chapter 1

Amusement Park Mecca

"Do you want a margarita?" yelled the insipidly chirpy waitress in the Hawaiian shirt. We were in the Jimmy Buffett–themed restaurant at Universal Studios, Orlando, and she was trying to be heard over "Come Monday," which was blaring from the speaker system.

"No," I said wearily. My feet throbbed, and, as the designated pack mule, I'd been lugging the twenty-pound backpack with the camera, extra batteries and chargers, water, fleeces, and enough snacks to outfit an Everest expedition. I'd been so distracted getting everyone else breakfast that morning that I hadn't had more than a few bites of the kids' cold toast. My blood sugar level was alarmingly low. I was ready to drink the ketchup right out of the crusty red bottle on the table.

"Really . . . ?" The waitress sounded genuinely surprised, almost disdainful. "You sure you don't want a margarita?"

What I said was "No thank you." What I really wanted to do was to grab her by the front of her fluorescent shirt with one fist, like they did in spaghetti westerns, and snarl, "Listen, *amiga,* you see these four kids here? You think I can possibly deal with this theme park and all four of them if I start downing tequila? Do you *want* me to blow chunks on the Hulk? Would you like me to pass out here in Margaritaville and lose this brood somewhere between Seuss Landing and Fear Factor Live?"

Instead, I kept my voice even, my countenance beaming, and an adoring look focused on my kids. I didn't want them to suspect for a moment that I wasn't as ecstatic as they were to be there. I'd shouldered the responsibility of continually making sure everyone was in tow, of keeping all four kids contented despite age gaps greater than the drop at Splash Mountain, determined that they view me as "Most Fun Mom." I wanted them to remember that I'd cheerily gone on all the rides with them, from Jimmy Neutron's Nicktoon Blast to the Amazing Adventures of Spider-Man. I wanted it seared in their brains that I'd let them order chocolate sundaes from room service and stay up late with in-room movies. I was focused on creating a fond memory so that, on my deathbed, they could all recall the time I'd loosened the purse strings and let them buy souvenirs and eat unlimited amounts of greasy park food. This was downright radical compared to our normal household rules.

I knew enough to understand that it would be years before the day-to-day martyrdom of mothering would even hit their radar screens. The nutritious home-cooked dinners, the homework patrol, and the midnight snuggles when they had the flu that made up the real heroics of parenting didn't earn medals. Those acts wouldn't truly be appreciated until my kids had children of their own and were bleeding out of their ears from the decibel level on an elementary school field-trip bus ride.

What they would *remember,* what would live in the collective film library of their childhood memories, was the highlight reel: the trips to Magic Kingdom, the ski weekends, and the beach vacations. The rest of it, the work in the trenches, would be like background noise; it was low-level radar, like the commercials in between the Oscar presentations. I needed to make this one big.

. . .

Our country's theme parks are the proving ground for parental excellence. I've yet to meet a mom or dad who has been able to escape a pilgrimage to Disney, Universal, Six Flags, or any of the other über-intense, megapacked square miles of finger-lickin' Fun for the Whole Family. Folks will clip coupons, hunt for bargains, look for deals, and save for years—anything to cross that threshold for the kids and snap those cherished family photos with Mickey or Buzz Lightyear with a giant roller coaster in the background.

But the pages in our family album wouldn't have the whole picture. My husband would need to be Photoshopped into the frame because, once again, right before the trip he had been sent on assignment to cover some world event; what had been planned as a family vacation had ended up as a milestone in single parenting. The responsibility, plus the twenty-pound backpack, was now on my Sherpa shoulders.

So here I was, alone with four kids: Mack, age sixteen, Cathryn, nearly fourteen, and twins Nora and Claire, who were seven. This was my big weekend in Orlando, where I was determined to prove that I was, in fact, the best mom in the world.

I felt the promise this one day had to erase all the recent failures: the moments when I had been distracted, or hadn't read to the twins at bedtime, or had spent too much time on my e-mail. There was always so much more I *could* be doing, *should* be doing if I was to be a GREAT mom.

So far we had braved threatening thunderclouds, pouring rain, and then blistering humidity. No wonder the park had been quiet and the lines not too long; we'd been soaked through to our footwear, and the weight on my back had felt ten pounds heavier. I had become an extra in *Saving Private Ryan*. As the afternoon had worn on, though, the sun had emerged, and masses of people began pushing through the turnstiles in all of their exuberant glory, as if Oprah herself had announced her giant giveaway sweepstakes. It seemed that everyone had a shot at the shiny red Chevrolet if they poured through the gates right now.

We'd snagged the last available table in the Jimmy Buffett restaurant and were soon digging into a coma-inducing amount of food: obese hamburgers, fries like fence posts, nachos dripping with cheese and jalapeños, sheer excess. This was vacation food, designed to stop arterial blood in its tracks. The "Volcano" song began blasting over the speakers, and some sort of earsplitting alarm with lights went off in the restaurant as a giant papier-mâché volcano began to smoke and froth. Soon green margarita water was running down the mountain and into a huge swirling goblet poised over the bar, reminiscent of Linda Blair in *The Exorcist*. My kids were transfixed. I was catatonic.

On the giant TV screens of the all-Buffett, all-the-time Sirius radio simulcast, men in silly shark-shaped foam hats holding up beers and women in what looked like a perimenopausal wet T-shirt contest with unspeakable sayings scrawled on their chests danced across the screen, wagging everything that was waggable. It looked like a colossal episode of *Grandparents Gone Wild*.

"Mom, what's wrong with those ladies?" Claire asked. Mack just smiled with an "I've seen it all before" teenage look. Lord knows what movies and Internet sites he had feasted on, out from under my watchful gaze.

"Those ladies are drunk," I said, using my weary church lady voice. "And that makes them do really stupid things." I was eager to change the subject.

My two younger children were getting a far earlier education in the marginal areas of life than the older ones had. Was I just worn down or simply inured? Or was it harder to rear two younger ones on good guy/bad guy morality tales when there were older siblings in the house? The teenagers understood that there could be gray areas and room for little white lies. My parental explanation skills had to span Barney to blow jobs, the colors of the rainbow to, ahem, rainbow parties. (Note to reader: if you need an explanation here, ask your teens. On second thought, don't ask your teens.) Come to think of it, a theme park was one of the few places where I could pretty much guarantee that everybody would be happy. Most of the time. If only I could keep track of them.

My defenses weaken in an amusement park. My normally high threshold for saying no lowers just enough for my kids to climb over the fence, and this, unfortunately, applies to more than greasy food. Perhaps that is just what the owners count on. Fatigue, exhaustion, the beating sun, or rain—it's almost easier to hand over the wallet than to fight the good fight. *Oh, what the heck,* I think to myself as Cathryn works on me for a hammered leather bracelet I know she will never wear again. "We're on vacation," I say with false cheer. This seems to mean that all of my rules are out the window. I'm now rolling with it.

With each turn through the fantastically constructed "lands" of the park there were endless opportunities for food and merchandising. I remained strong as we passed numerous booths for great globs of fried dough the size of a large pizza. Big and small people passed me gnawing on giant caveman-sized turkey legs like packs of wolves, ripping the pink meat with their teeth as they shambled forward like extras in *Night of the Living Dead.*

Spider-Man mugs, key chains with our names on them, flip-flops with SpongeBob's head; in my cheeseburger-and-roller-coaster-induced trance I told myself we would probably never be here again, so it was okay to buy some mementos. I found myself peeling off more bills, even though I knew with certainty that these items would end up in the garage-sale basket or church thrift shop by spring cleaning. These tchotchkes would be cherished for exactly one day and then become prime candidates for my famous biannual "crap control" efforts as I swept through the house with industrial-sized black garbage bags.

"Can I have this necklace?" my daughter Nora asked sweetly. It was some kind of sea-themed monstrosity from the *Jaws* ride, distantly related to the ubiquitous pukka shells popular in my teens, when an "authentic" strand of pukka was the height of chic. Where had they found all these pukkas? What the heck *was* a pukka?

Meanwhile, I was fascinated by my son's approach to the park, something he had looked forward to for a long time. He walked a few paces behind us, continually texting up-to-the-minute info about each ride to his friends back home on his cell phone. He was becoming a kind of real-time information booth on which rides were cool, which ones were "duds," and what we simply *had* to do while we were here.

It took all I had not to be a mom as I watched this. I fought the urge to say, "Put away the electronics, kiddo, and just enjoy this . . . be in the moment." Because, in fact, he was in the moment. This was how our kids did moments now; they multitasked and instant-messaged through some of the great moments in life, one eye on the keyboard and one on real time. I had to remind myself that just because it was different from how I'd processed experiences as a kid, it didn't make it wrong. I held my tongue and took a bite of Cathryn's red licorice to settle the cheeseburger.

As we walked through the park's uncanny versions of lower Manhattan, Wall Street, and San Francisco's Fishermen's Wharf, I marveled at how sophisticated amusement parks had become. Why bother to actually visit all these places separately when you could just come here? You'd save a fortune on airfare and hotels.

Growing up in upstate New York, my sisters and I had thought that the height of excitement was a visit to Storytown in Lake George Village. I remember the real-life Cinderella in the pumpkin carriage and her magical dress with cut-glass beads. There was the Frontier Town train ride chugging slowly through the badlands. Although I could see the unpainted boards on the back of the two-dimensional saloon, and the bandit mechanically popped up on cue when the little train chugged around the boulder, it was all simply magical.

Before computer generation, before elaborate headset video games, Steven Spielberg, and holographic special effects, our expectations were so reasonable, so minimal that I was simply bamboozled by that long-ago theme park.

Did my kids feel transported today? It would be hard to compare.

They had each become such jaded, sophisticated consumers, flooded daily with images and transported by sensational, three-dimensional simulation.

Still, no matter how elaborate and lifelike the graphics and holograms got, it seemed there was no substitute for good old-fashioned Newton-defying physics to get the kids riled up. This was evident from the screams as I found myself in line for the Hulk rollercoaster, a giant green monster of rails and poles that thundered over the top of the walkway, twisting like a worm on dry pavement with scores of terrified riders.

"It's going to be so cool to go totally upside down," said Mack. I'm not much of a meat eater, so the giant cheeseburger in paradise was still objecting at every turn of my digestive system. My mother says this is her food "reporting back to her." I remembered seeing something that week on TV about a ground beef recall, the biggest in history. My first cheeseburger in months and it could be contaminated meat from a theme park. I eyed the screaming riders corkscrewing above me.

As we approached the Hulk, a sign with a yardstick indicating the required height stood prominently by the entrance. My twins fell a good five inches short.

Seeing this, Claire huffed and began to wail. Unlike her more Zen-like twin sister, she was caught between two worlds. She wanted desperately to be as grown up as her fourteen-year-old sister and sixteen-year-old brother, yet she milked her "youngest" status in the family for every last drop.

"I want to go on the Hulk," she said, crossing her arms over her chest and thrusting out her lower lip. "Why can't I go? Why do I have to be that tall?" *Sigh.*

As the four of us tried to reason with her, she sat down by the entrance and put her head in her hands. I had a lose-lose scenario here: ride with my sixteen-year-old or mollify my crying second grader. Mack had a year left in our home before college, I reflected, and this might be the last roller-coaster ride of our lives together. Nostalgia and reason won out. I chose the ride with Mack, leaving the twins behind with a grim-faced Cathryn, who had no interest in the belly-lurching experience.

Once we were strapped into a chair with so much padding I thought we might be going intergalactic, the Hulk took off slowly, then, on the incline, instantly achieved warp speed. I couldn't even turn my head to see how Mack, next to me, was doing. All I could do was scream like Tippi Hedren as each turn buffeted me against the halter, speed instantly peeling my lips inside out while the centrifugal force plastered me back against the seat. I had a flashback of my first time in Disney World as a teenager, when the It's a Small World attraction became stuck and we were trapped inside a room of costumed dolls singing the song repeatedly in twenty languages. That had actually been more terrifying than this roller coaster, I thought.

As the Hulk began its first lightning-quick upside-down roll, I felt the cheeseburger with mushrooms and hot sauce preparing its first report. Screaming, I struggled for control of my digestive system, wondering how many people's stomachs released their contents with a little coaxing from the Hulk. Who would it land on if I lost it? What was the trajectory of vomit at 100 circular miles per hour?

When the ride was over, momentarily unable to speak, I climbed out of the seat and wobbled down the ramp, my eyes rolling in different directions, lips so parched I couldn't form words. Mack, on the other hand, couldn't have been more thrilled and immediately resumed texting.

After the Mummy and the Spider-Man rides, my head and internal organs still spinning, we were forced to split into two groups, older and younger. Claire was still sniffling about the height requirement, so I shamelessly bought both twins a bucket of blue cotton candy, which they proceeded to smear all over themselves and somehow tangle in my hair.

This was how I found myself in line in Poseidon's temple holding two empty plastic canisters. "Girls, follow me," I whispered loudly as our simulated safari-outfitted "guide" in the temple found a secret passage out through the parting of the sea.

"Wash your hands in the water—quick," I said in hushed tones. "Stick them in the fountain but don't lick them." I figured there were a lot worse things in that swirling water than cotton candy juice. It most likely carried bacteria from every continent, and God knew what sorts of *E. coli* contaminants. We waited until most of the crowd of Poseidon's captives had gone through and I felt as guilty as if I were teaching my children to steal penny candy from the open grocery store bins. I furtively tried to lift their hands into the waterfall, falling short by just a few inches, and I looked around to make sure there was no hidden camera. I vowed never to leave home without towelettes again.

As I contemplated this latest symptom of single parenting, my cell phone rang. It was my husband, calling from North Korea. It had been a few days since he'd been able to get through to me. He was exhausted and jet-lagged and dragged down by some virulent strain of winter flu.

"You sound tired," I said.

"Where are you?" he asked. "You're breaking up."

I belted out, "I'm in Poseidon's temple." The woman with the oversized designer sunglasses in front of me turned to shoot me a disgusted look.

"You're what?" He sounded exhausted. I could hear in his voice a tinge of guilt that, once again, the demands of reporting had taken him away from a planned family vacation.

"Poseidon's temple!" I yelled, which made no sense to him. "But never mind." It was midnight in North Korea. Owing to bad weather and missed connections, he told me, it had taken him multiple extra flights to get there.

"I'm in Universal Studios with the kids," I said, patiently starting over, though he should have known this already, if we were on his radar at all. I could hear my own voice echo across the satellite. "I'll bet you wish you were me right now."

As the connection finally cut out, I eyed the conga line of parents with their various accessories: strollers and sippy cups, muffin tops and beer bellies, video cameras and baseball caps. This was America in every flavor and hue.

An amusement park is a great place to people-watch. It is like a multicolored snow globe of American culture. It is the great leveler. We saw snobby-cheerleader moms in line next to gangbanging hipsters with jeans pushed down to mid-thigh. We watched giggling Japanese tourist teens with white knee socks and Hello Kitty plastic purses. There were the yellers, the screamers, the indulgers, and the arm yankers. We spied highly pierced punk rockers with spiked hair and combat boots. And of course there were people just like me with sensible shoes, out-of-style sunglasses, and bulging backpacks just "two steps away from a fanny pack," as my son had critically announced.

Explain to me the people who bring newborns to the park with no visible sign of older children in tow. Who are you kidding? The two-month-old has been begging to go on Terminator 2: 3-D? Is there a Jamba Juice stand with Similac at the food courts?

I saw tattoos and body art in more shapes and sizes and in stranger places on the body than I'd ever witnessed in one location. My twins pointed out a soccer mom with a cute blond bob who had a giant multicolored serpent twining around her entire calf. She was holding an infant in her arms and dragging two other small kids. "Brutal," my son remarked, raising an eyebrow over his cell phone.

"Mom, look at that guy's earlobes," Cathryn said, aghast. The young Goth with the huge chain dragging out of his back pocket had put holes in his lobes and inserted what looked like large rings—so that if you stared at him straight on it was like gazing through a giant viewfinder at the vista behind him.

"Don't stare, honey," I cautioned. Did they have metal detectors in theme parks? What color was the terrorist threat in a place like this?

"That's disgusting," Claire said in a very loud voice.

. . .

By about five P.M., the thrill of being a pack mule and the answer-woman Girl Guide all day was wearing thin. The bar back at Margaritaville was all of a sudden looking incredibly enticing. Maybe the perky waitress at lunch really had had the right idea after all. Perhaps, in the end, she'd seen enough parents with kids here to know that alcohol was in fact the only answer at a theme park.

Those cheerful people at the bar by the barf-green margarita-rupturing volcano: maybe they truly understood that in order to survive and let go, you needed to anesthetize yourself.

Perhaps that was what other parents did here. They numbed out. They got enough antifreeze in their systems to make them immune to the tugs on the sleeves, the eighteenth time they almost tripped as their kid cluelessly cut right in front of them.

Perhaps a mixing bowl–sized beer mug was the key to evenhandedly tackling the seventh quest for the bathroom and the never-ending lines among people who were prime candidates for a fresh swipe of pine-scented deodorant.

"Don't touch me," I growled under my breath as some big lummox in a Celtics shirt unexpectedly hurtled toward me, pushed by his chortling sidekick, and narrowly missed stepping on my foot. What was happening to me? I wondered. It was my cut-off time for humanity. I'd hit my limit. I had a vision of what I would do to the next person who crossed me. I would take a rope of Cathryn's red licorice and jump on their back, quickly hog-tie their hands and feet, and stand triumphantly on their body like a great white hunter.

By the end of the day I had almost vomited on the roller coaster, superheroes and bad guys had shot fire at us, and we'd been snatched from the jaws of death in Twister and terrified by Mummies. We'd had constant, throbbing stimulation, like rats on acid, and we'd reached our fill of performances by chirpy, overcaffeinated wanna-be actors in the roles of their lifetimes.

Tired but satisfied, all five of us strolled out of the park at sunset, just as it closed, to find the bus to our hotel. Right outside the park doors a whole new nightlife was heating up, with live bands, Mardi Gras beads, food, bars, and other mind-numbing attractions. No chance, guys: we were beyond temptation. The kids' earlier demands to go back the next day had given way to a feeling that they were satisfied. They had done all the rides they had set out to do. Except for Claire, who was still in a low-level smolder.

She huffed in the bus seat next to me, dramatically clamping her arms in front of her chest, as she'd no doubt learned from countless young Mary-Kate and Ashley videos.

"When am I going to be tall enough?" she fumed. "When? You can't say you promise I will and then be wrong."

"You will be tall enough someday, I know," I said. "That is true. I just don't know how fast you will grow. I can't tell you exactly when."

"But I want to ride the Hulk," she said.

"I know, sweetheart. I know."

"So we have to come back," she demanded. "I want to come back. And to Epcot and SeaWorld too. Promise?"

"I promise," I said. And the congealed remains of the giant Jimmy Buffett cheeseburger and red licorice did a little flip-flop in my stomach, as I understood that a promise was a promise. This wasn't something I could welsh on. This wasn't something she would forget. Every kid deserves the chance to see Mickey, I reasoned. Every kid deserves the chance to battle the Hulk roller coaster.

"Pinkie swear?" she said.

"Pinkie swear," I answered. And we put up our pinkies and entwined them as the bus rolled along the highway in the disappearing Florida sunlight.

After all, Bob had sat this one out, and he, too, deserved a chance to ride the Hulk.

Chapter 2

Adolescence

At some point the curtain comes down on the ringside seats to our children's developmental milestones. Put simply, the bathroom door slams shut. The body that was once your province to explore freely, to examine every inch of for tiny imperfections—freckles, chicken pox, scratches, ticks—is off-limits.

They were my babies, to bathe, to tickle toes and blow on tummies. The snuggling and loving then was on my terms. It was physical and tactile and I couldn't touch them enough. Now my kids grab for towels or throw their arms across their bodies as if they've been caught in a Saturday morning walk of shame out of a fraternity house.

I get glimpses of my older daughter as she races from the bathroom, having forgotten something, clutching her chest strategically, like Jean Valjean gripping the bread in *Les Misérables*. As for my son, I can only guess at the details surrounding the arrival of puberty, based on his

ever-dropping voice and the hairy tree trunks that poke out of his comforter when I wake him for school.

Our open family policy of unintentional nudity has ended. We used
to not make a big deal about our bodies. We didn't run a suburban nud-
ist colony; we didn't parade around the kitchen in the buff. But we had
one of those unwritten rules that if someone happened to spot us in
the bedroom, or pop in when we were in the shower, it was no big deal.
We didn't lock doors, and we tried to be as nonchalant as possible if
one of the kids walked in. There were times when I could feel my children's eyes boring into the parts of my body that I might want to improve, minimize, or, in one area, expand. I'd pay money to have heard
the little bubbles of thoughts inside their heads at those moments. Or
maybe not.

Mommy has a tummy, Mommy is saggy, Mommy has a jiggly butt—
who knows what horrors those little eyes were seeing as they edged
toward their own changes, becoming ever more critical of me.

"You have to wear pajamas," my daughter commanded my husband
recently on the premises of our bedroom. "I don't want to see you
naked," she added with a slight twinkle. "It's gross."

"Well, then don't come look," Bob answered good-naturedly. But
he's been sleeping with pajama bottoms ever since. Suddenly, in our
household, everybody is a critic, and Bob and I seem to be under some
kind of prison-yard klieg lighting, as if our home has been turned into
an operating room.

I had grown up in a house accepting of unintentional nakedness
and had wanted to make a sincere effort to demonstrate to my own
kids that bodies were just that—bodies. They were natural and normal
and "everybody has one." I will say that I was one of three daughters,
with no brothers, and there were many moments when we happened
to accidentally stumble across Dad getting out of the shower. Playing
doctor was boring with a sister, so it was our only chance to spot a real,
live male penis. Of course, the whole experience at age six or eight was

truly disgusting, and we made the appropriate gagging motions in our rooms after our hasty, giggling escapes.

Now with a boy and girl in the midst of serious adolescence, the bathroom door is sealed tighter than a government nuclear testing ground in New Mexico. Sullenness, eye rolling, and maximum displays of embarrassment have reached Oscar-worthy performance levels in our house. Yet lying just a few layers below that toughened epidermis are my two awkward older children, testing their capacity to demonstrate love while being buffeted by a million little hormones swimming against the current.

And now, after years of wishing they would just sleep in, I cannot seem to rouse them without multiple attempts and my "outside voice." I am the zookeeper in the lions' den. It might go easier for me if I just opened the door and tossed in a slab of red meat first to soften them up before I entered.

With one eye on the clock, my first strategy involves a little affectionate snuggling, usually with the response of faint groans. The second attempt is the flicked on overhead light, kind of like I'm the warden in juvi. The third journey up the stairs from the kitchen involves loud yelling, though not too loud or it will wake the twins, who will otherwise sleep for another half hour while I wrestle and wrench their older siblings out the door to high school. I have never had to use the fourth attempt, but I imagine that it would involve a blunt instrument.

The other day I went in to wake up my teenage son. As I ruffled his hair, whispered in his ear, and then rubbed his back, my hand wandered inadvertently down to his butt. His tiny baby butt, the one I used to diaper and tickle and marvel at the perfection of, adoring those two mini hemispheres as I bathed him.

For a brief second I thought about the hours when his little baby body was mine alone. I remembered how my husband and I had discovered a minuscule hole, an indentation really, just above Mack's left ear that the doctor said was a long-ago relic of evolution that simply hadn't closed all the way during natal development: a tiny speck no one but a mother or a lover would notice.

With new motherhood came all of the fears of loss, disease, injury, and even kidnapping. I comforted myself with the idea that if Mack was ever taken, the little tiny imperfection above his ear would be my identifying mark, far more certain than a fingerprint or an eye color. It was Bob's and my secret, our collective handiwork.

As I stood there in my reverie, my hand on his comforter, suddenly, like the swamp thing in a horror movie . . . it was *alive*.

"Moooooommmm!" he snarled, rolling away, horrified that his mother had been fondling his fanny, if ever so briefly. For a split second I thought I'd try to explain to him that no matter how big and hairy, smelly, and manlike he got, I would always see that little baby butt when he hung suspended between sleep and wakefulness. I would always picture my little man standing on his tiptoes in the crib in his dinosaur Onesies, calling to me at some indecent hour to come get him out. But when you're sixteen, that kind of nostalgia just doesn't play. Especially at seven A.M. on a school day.

When was it exactly that they crossed the time zone from begging to build Duplo towers with me and wanting to stir the batter to being intensely private, often brooding beasts who quickly clear the computer screen when I walk into the room?

With each one of my four children I can vividly remember that first pediatrician visit, when, like a bunch of bananas, they were weighed on a tiny scale, marking a new entry in the baby book.

In that first year as parents, we conduct minute inspections. During bath time we discover the new mosquito bite, marvel at the little wrinkles on their wrists and the dimples on their knuckles. We watch hair come in and eyes fix their color. As the years tick on, we buy new shoes at more regular intervals and watch the size turn from 12 to 1. We move from the 18 months section at Baby Gap to single-digit sizes, and we retire pacifiers and sell changing tables at garage sales.

We go from getting ambushed with pee during those early diaper changes to praying that they will be smart enough one day to use condoms. We watch chamois-soft faces become a painful terrain of pimples as a hormonal tempest wrestles beneath the skin like the forces of good and evil. We transition from toilet-training target practice (we had our son try to hit floating Cheerios) to mortification about anything relating to bodily smells or functions (except jokes about poop). Where I once was sort of a right-hand mom, directing the flow during potty training, now I am a pariah, the lowest form of human life when it comes to matters involving private parts or morphing bodies. And it is at this point, before we are ready and before we can process it all, that the bathroom door shuts us out once and for all.

My own adolescence was garden-variety painful, forged by the singular experience of being just about the absolute last person in my grade to develop.

I remember buying a training bra long before I really needed one and willing my boobs to bud. Life back then wasn't all that different from life now. In those early adolescent years, it seemed most male attention was focused on the girls who had matured. It was all about breasts.

My memories of myself are of a painfully thin girl with stick-straight blond hair. The clothes that defined that era—the 1970s—did little to help me along in the fashion circles. Striped Danskin polyester shirts and matching pants, maxi dresses, bell-bottoms as wide as a hoopskirt—these were part of the uniform of the decade.

Pirate's dream (sunken chest), carpenter's dream (flat as a board and easy to nail)—these are the nicknames from the boys I remember vividly. And I laughed and smiled on the outside, determined to be a good sport, vowing there would be no evidence of just how sharp those barbs were internally.

In fifth grade the mysterious movie *The Yellow Dress* was shown, only to the girls; we were ushered into the cafeteria as the boys were sent to the gym to play dodgeball.

The Yellow Dress was a stiffly acted, 1950s industrial-style film about a girl who wanted to buy a shapely yellow dress she saw in the window of a store. At the time, her body hadn't yet filled out enough for it, and she was disappointed. But lo and behold, with a little nutrition and proper hygiene, puberty took root, and darn it all if that yellow dress didn't finally fit in time for the big dance.

I recall stark black-and-white diagrams and explanations of menstruation, something that would be years away for me. But what I remember most was the chant the boys took up as we filed back out of the cafeteria. "Bleeders . . . bleeders," they began to yell. And in the kind of mass female hysteria typically associated with previous centuries or Beatles concerts, a number of the girls began to cry, a response that bewildered me. The exchange was dramatic and in some ways mysterious, musky and ripe with the hint of sexual tension to come.

So much about being accepted as an adolescent revolves around looks: the right clothes, the same hair, the brand names, the cool sneakers. Today it seems to be the Uggs over the no-name version, the right kind of blue jean, tight and peg-legged this month, but with a flare last year. Long hair is now all the rage for girls. As a mother I must constantly try to be apprised of the little nuances, all the little details that, if you aren't paying attention, you just might miss. And that would be the sin of "uncoolness."

In my house, in the secret recesses of the bathroom, the mirror reigns supreme. As I once pored over every inch of their bodies, they now do that for themselves. My oldest daughter inspects every hair, each freckle, and tiny imperfection.

"Mooooommm, do you see this white part?" my daughter yells to me, waving me over to an area on the small of her back, one that only a contortionist could have gotten to in the first place. How did she even see this little patch of skin when I can barely make it out myself? Even when I get my 1.75 reading glasses I decide I will need a *CSI*-style forensics kit to properly examine it. "Why won't it tan?" she asks.

I marvel at the kind of time required to be an adolescent. While I'm worrying about what's for dinner, which bills are overdue, and how I will get four children to three separate extracurricular activities, she gets to carefully study every millimeter of her body. My teenagers are now programmed to dawdle and luxuriate. Their very beings operate in a different time zone—heck, a different stratosphere. *Enjoy this now*, I think, with a degree of sick satisfaction, *because you won't ever get to do it again.*

The shower runs constantly these days. The smallest physical exertions require "freshening up." It might be easier to just install a waterfall. I think back to when I used to have to cajole my daughter to shower after four days. When I feared that she could grow up to be a human pigpen, trailing her own marinade of dirt and alarming smells. Somewhere in the tween years the gene for extreme personal hygiene kicked in. Ultrahypervigilant cleanliness became the modus operandi on the second floor. She was on patrol for the slightest nub on her legs or any eyebrow hairs in need of a quick tweeze.

My teenage son, never what I'd call a big talker, has morphed into a Mr. Hyde; Mr. Grunt and Grumpy, I'll call him. Like a groundhog, all at once he'll poke his head out of the hole to grace us with a sentence fragment.

I get the whole eye-rolling treatment big-time from everyone. Even my eight-year-olds have gotten in the game now, exposed early on to the condemnation of their older siblings. They've all read the memo on how to belittle *and* annoy Mom. There is serious strength in numbers.

"Mom, you're embarrassing me," says Claire when I dance in the kitchen or sing along with the car radio. Nothing I do is right; some days my clothes are too frumpy, other days too revealing. I serve leftovers, force feed Brussels sprouts, and listen to cheesy satellite radio stations. I'm too tired, I'm too joyous, or I'm too silly. I yell out of car windows at my friends when I'm happy to see them; my children stiffen and crumple down in the backseat. During daylight hours and most assuredly anytime in public, I am dog doo on the sole of a shoe.

I think of my children like sea turtles in Florida that must hatch out of their eggs and persevere on their journey to the shoreline by following the pull of the moon. These days, Cathryn is fighting her own hormonally programmed urges. Part of this ancient ritual and rite of passage includes being disgusted by your own horribly uncool parents.

One July night last year in our close-knit Adirondack summer community there was a local band playing. Out in an open field, the sun had set and the sky near the lake had taken on that purplish, rosy hue. A few figures danced by a fire, others played beach volleyball, and one lone woman swayed in a kind of Woodstock trance. Cathryn and a few of her friends stood around taking it all in, deciding how to posture themselves, feeling out if it was okay to dance.

I grabbed my longtime girlfriend Liza, the one I had snuck my first alcoholic drink with (vodka and OJ), and we began to cut loose to a '70s tune. We dropped our mom masks and suddenly we were sixteen again, at an open-air Eagles concert. As our silliness escalated and we spun into crazier gyrating moves, dipping each other and swivel-hipping like Elvis, Cathryn came running over to me, a look of panic contorting her face.

"Mom!" she admonished. "Cut it out. Stop it now!" She seized my arm and tried to physically haul me off the field.

Laughing, Liza and I said our good-byes as I packed up my kids and headed to the car. A bat swooped low over our heads and the last traces of the sun had vanished, almost erasing the line where the mountains met the lake. It was a magical time of the evening, the gloaming, my favorite hour.

As we approached the car I began to cut loose again, dancing wildly, kicking my feet in the air like I'd caught Lucky Charms. With my twins giggling and imitating me, Cathryn tried to keep her stone face disapproving, but my moves were so ridiculous, so idiotic, that she couldn't help but crack a smile. As she continued to drag me toward the car by my arm, we both began to laugh and then she, too, began to dance.

All of the impulses she had suppressed on the field with her friends, all of the budding desires her legs had had to move to the music, came bursting forth and we both danced hilariously in exaggerated movements for few moments, finally falling onto the grass in a fit of giggles.

I would endure a lifetime of criticism for wearing a baggy sweatshirt, a thong at my age, or being too boisterous in the school parking lot to have experienced just one of these moments in the field with my daughter. And I will hold that image in my mind long after she has left the house and begun a family of her own.

That night, in the calm of the tuck-in ritual before bed, I watched my judgmental teenager become her loving self again, the little girl who doesn't want to let me down.

"I'm sorry for today," she said, snuggling me closer to her, and I could feel the thickness of her ponytail in my hands; the hair that used to be so scraggly, the hair I worried would always be wisps.

"What are you sorry about?" I said, the multiple verbal infarctions, the rolling eyes and disgusted actions all forgiven. Lying in bed with her arms thrust out to me she was four or five again, eager for a goodnight embrace to banish the day's challenges.

"I'm sorry I was mean to you," she said, and she pulled me closer for a kiss.

Chapter 3

The Friendship Zone

Melanie and I are survivors. We have endured the death of her husband in Iraq and the grievous injury of mine. In the months following David's death, I was there to relieve the day-to-day realities of decisions and living while she grappled and grieved. She, in turn, was there with an eternal kindness and steely strength when my tank was lower than empty. She held my hope on days when Bob lay in a medically induced coma, his wrists tied with restraints so that he would not pull out the many tubes crisscrossing his body.

After Bob was injured in the war by a roadside bomb, I jokingly referred to Melanie and myself as "D & D," or "Death" (Mel) and "Dismemberment" (me). We were not exactly the two people you most wanted to have at your next dinner party. We were better company with just each other.

I got the call about David early one Sunday April morning. It was his employer, NBC News; they couldn't reach Melanie and they had information, they said, to tell her about David. He was embedded with the army as they advanced toward the invasion of Baghdad, and all of America seemed to be fascinated with watching the war on TV. My husband was with a marine division just twelve miles from David. She and I had both been on edge. We had ended up talking daily to each other on the phone, trading information and news from our husbands if we had gotten calls that day or received precious e-mails.

I knew from the tone of the voice on the phone that the news could not be good. I reached Mel and told her to hang on; I would dress quickly and drive to her house, a few towns away. It was during that drive over backcountry roads, before I reached her, that I learned that David was gone, suddenly; he had collapsed in the sand.

In those moments, in the hush of her sleeping home, she was learning of her husband's collapse and then death from a blood clot that had been snaking its way up his leg from a bruise he'd gotten on a tank. Her world, and that of her girls, would be first shattered and then forever changed.

Three years after that, it was my phone that rang. My husband's boss had tracked me down. Ironically, someone at ABC News had called Melanie to find me, also early in the morning, with my cell phone turned off in a hotel room in Disney World. Melanie knew, before I did, that something was wrong, and this knowledge had reignited the fuse of terror and grief that had smoldered within her since after David's passing.

These calls, these connections, would shape us forever, twin us in tragedy, even though our stories would have different angles and vastly different outcomes.

Driving toward Melanie's side after David's sudden death, I'd felt my world shrink down to a pinprick containing the singular shock of this information. I thought only of getting to her, not of the next day or the months afterward or the thousands of hours of grief we would all collectively endure. It didn't occur to me until weeks later that the very fabric of our friendship would change. The events and emotions that would unfold would, in a way, bind us to each other forever.

David was a young and strapping reporter, engaged and more alive than most people I knew. He felt life with every neuron and processed it viscerally. His loss rippled through many communities of friends and colleagues, but it tore through the heart of his family like a bullet.

In those days and weeks following that news, the world seemed, all at once, frozen, without mirth or light. The outcome of what had happened, the unfathomable tragedy and ache of loss, would make each day feel wet and heavy.

We spent hours after David died sitting alone by the fireplace in Mel's bedroom, hugging our knees to our chests. There, in the capricious northeastern weather of early April, a snowstorm whipped up, as if highlighting our grief. On some of those days I held Mel, as a mother comforts her children, and I forced her to eat and drink. I tried to assure her that, despite this overwhelming horror, in the end, I knew she would survive. As hollow as my words felt at the time, it was purely the being there that counted, like sitting shivah. In those days I was a soft-spoken warm body and a set of strong, confident arms. There is little that makes you feel as helpless as a loved one's pain.

David's death created a void, a giant sinkhole into which life, happiness, and laughter was sucked for a long time. A death leaves emptiness, a vast expanse—the person is suddenly gone forever. And grief can simply paralyze you, freeze your bones in place and numb your mind into a film loop that replays the what-ifs.

I could try to fill some of that void with my presence, by laughing and joking, by listening and cajoling. I told her I would always be there and that I loved her. Love was powerful medicine after a loss, I learned, yet it still fell short. The person who had loved her the most was irretrievably gone. I watched and waited as searing grief gave way to habitual mourning and Mel slowly, gradually, entered the land of the living at her own pace, sometimes advancing timidly and then retreating when it all felt like too much.

Then it was my turn. When I got that first call from ABC about Bob's tank and crew being hit by a bomb in Iraq, Mel reached me by phone minutes after. "I'm coming with you to Germany to see Bob in the military hospital," she said to me. "And you cannot stop me. You were there for me every step of the way, and I'm going to be there for you."

We flew to Landstuhl, Germany, to see what was left of Bob after the explosion had blown off his helmet, crushed his skull, and left him lying lifeless and cold. She sat next to me on the plane, pressing my hand when she saw my thoughts drifting out the window, circling the black hole of terror that lurked just below my brittle patina of calm.

"What do you think we will find there?" I asked her. I was scared and trembling, like a small child who needed a parent.

"I think we will find a man who is hurt and needs to heal, but he will come back."

I knew she was telling me what I wanted to hear, but sometimes that is also the great strength of a good girlfriend. There are moments when forced cheer does the trick, moments when white lies are the kindest approach.

"Look at me, Lee," Mel said, drawing my clenched fist into the palms of her hands. "I am the worst-case scenario. We lost David, and yet the girls and I have survived. We got through the absolute worst of it and we are still here."

I had to agree that the suddenness of the way David had died was a stunning trip wire—the lack of warning of his deep vein thrombosis, the fact that it might have been prevented if we'd known the symptoms, if we'd gotten him out of there. The bruise on the leg, the cramped conditions of sleeping in the tank, the exhaustion, the dehydration—knowledge of any of this could have saved his life. In retrospect, the not knowing had been its own form of torture for Mel, her own horrible movie trailer that had looped over and over in her head for many weeks and months after he died.

"Where there is life, there is hope," she said to me. She held my gaze as if it could give me strength, fortify me for what my eyes would see when we landed: the gruesome sight of a loved one blown apart by a bomb, clinging to life and consigned to an uncertain fate.

But I wasn't sure if I agreed with her, if what she said was true. On some level I imagined that death might ultimately be cleaner. If Bob's fate was to be so incapacitated that I would be taking four children to visit their once vivid father in a nursing home each week, I didn't know then if I wanted Bob to live on those terms. That scenario was terrifying, and the thoughts hung with guilt as I stuffed them back down. I would need to stay in a world of hope and faith. That kind of negative thinking would have no value during this limbo. So I listened to Mel, and I let her hope soothe me. I would learn to walk a tightrope with my eyes squeezed shut, holding on to the hands of my friends and family. I would not look down, would not contemplate the possibility of anything short of getting to the other side, the side where Bob was alive, awake, and well.

Those were raw days for each of us in sequence, those years when Mel and I took turns with our grief. We would do things for each other, comfort each other in ways we could never have imagined when our friendship was young and fresh and full of endless possibilities and roads not yet taken.

Now she is a girlfriend of extremes, one with whom I have experienced both the unbearable weight and the joyful lightness of being. That kind of friendship is a priceless commodity; it exists in its own safety zone. And while it carries with it responsibility, it is also one of the greatest privileges I know.

When I think back to some of the very lowest moments in my life, they are ones I spent with Mel. Those kinds of experiences connect you in ways you cannot imagine until you have unintentionally tested a friendship by enduring a crisis together. I imagine this is why war veterans feel such a bond, why they meet as a group in VFW posts and for reunions and trips to the beach at Normandy, knowing that they alone can understand what it is they survived in the terrifying reality of combat. Only they understand what they lost and what they witnessed, even if they choose never to speak about it.

For all of those months of my grief and fear, Mel listened patiently, as girlfriends do. She didn't try to talk me out of it, didn't attempt to wedge me from my position; she sympathized, not minimized. When our conversation was over, I simply felt better, unburdened. Not jump-out-of-your-chair-and-do-calisthenics better, but just a modicum better. And sometimes a modicum is all a person needs.

When Bob was so gravely injured and our roles flip-flopped, I learned how different the tragedy of injury was from the tragedy of death. You do not have the luxury of falling apart; you must remain, in all of your waking moments, ever vigilant. There are decisions to make and doctors to talk to, there is an ever-gnawing fear that consumes you and there are often dire predictions, which you have to fight back. There are sorrowful family members around you and information to manage; people who need to know the status and others who must be kept at bay for fear that they will capsize you with their own grief.

When Melanie kept asking what she could do for me, it was so different from all those days when I had simply sat with her after David died. There was no sitting once Bob was injured. There was only a frantic vortex into which all normalcy was sucked. The way in which Melanie helped me was by shoring up the periphery, as I called it: taking my kids when they needed sleepovers, managing information to our mutual friends, and holding the hope for me on those days when that task seemed too heavy a load.

"I wish I could do more to help," Melanie told me more than a few times. "You gave up your life for me." And of course we both knew that was a misguided, if noble, emotion. Friendship should never be a quid pro quo. But I felt oddly guilty about the inequality, as if I needed to give her more to do. Sometimes all you can do is simply move forward through each new day.

On the occasion of my twin daughters' kindergarten play, I had been living in Bethesda by Bob's hospital bedside, waiting with his brothers and parents for him to emerge from his medically induced coma. I needed to fly home and enter my house for the first time since his injury. What had once been a bustling household, waiting for Dad to return from covering a story or reporting the news, was now a place I dreaded. Would it be the new site of a sickhouse? The home of a father and husband who was diminished somehow, crippled in the eyes of his children? The kitchen that we had remodeled only the summer before seemed shiny and new, too bright for the tenor of our now muted lives, the ones lived in the ICU, vacillating between hopefulness and despair.

During my first trip away from Bob, Melanie came down to the D.C. hospital to fill my shoes, as my sisters, close friends, and Bob's family had done for me during the hours when I needed to step away from his bedside.

With Melanie there, I knew that he would be tended to, that he would feel the sensation of a loving touch, somewhere in the recesses of his coma, and that she would gently push him back into bed over and over when he tried to blindly, rotely climb out. I knew that she would give him the same loving-kindness that I tried to lavish on him, so that somewhere inside his comatose but healing brain he would feel safe, loved, and eager to return to us.

As I headed back down to Washington after the kindergarten play—I'd sobbed my way through the performance, thinking about how much Bob would have wanted to be there—Melanie and I crossed paths at the airport. She was flying back home to her suburban New York town and I was returning to my post at Bob's bedside.

Sitting on a bench by baggage claim we stared out at the airport traffic through the glass wall. During those moments there was no one else in the airport, or so it felt.

"Why us, Mel?" I said dejectedly. "We were just minding our business, we weren't asking for too much, were we?" She had finished telling me that she believed Bob would be better and that he would return to reporting again, something that was difficult, in the bright light of day, to imagine after all of the medical pronouncements and his present, unresponsive condition.

"I don't know why, Lee," she answered, her voice growing softer as she became contemplative. "But I have you as my friend. And that gives me the strength to get up on those mornings when I want to roll over."

There is very little in life that can equal the rich, deep connective tissue of the committed, loving relationship of a good marriage. The years logged, the family created, the memories and shared experiences, the feeling that someone loves you despite your flaws and the parts they'd change if they could. All of these things had made me feel so completely whole married to Bob. But if I couldn't have them, if Bob were to have died in that hospital, or never have come back as a functioning person, I knew that I would have my children, my family, and the power of the friendship of girlfriends like Mel. They would all help to pull me back out into the light, eventually. And that was a mighty powerful feeling. It was much more than a consolation prize.

I can go for weeks without talking to Melanie and then I'll answer the phone and we'll pick up practically where we left off the last time. There is no preamble; no opening niceties are needed. Many times now we can finish each other's sentences, the way I do with my sisters. We've touched black and burned places in each other's souls, those spots we keep covered and bandaged away from others in our lives. They are too ugly to look at, too raw to gaze upon, and they are often best hidden from the other ones we love, the ones still bathed mostly in innocence.

Five years after David died, two years after our own horror, my family was sitting in a southwestern-style church in Santa Barbara. Our twins were flower girls, resplendent in gray silk dresses and silver shoes. It had rained for the better part of the day, but as we waited for the bride to appear, shards of sunlight magically shot through the upper windows of the church and fell on the baby Jesus in the Christmas crèche below as if it were a planned special effect.

Melanie appeared at the back of the church looking the way every bride is meant to look, radiant, fresh, excited, and slightly nervous. At the altar, Dan beamed with palpable emotion. My breath caught in my throat. I moved closer to Bob in the pew next to me and grabbed his hand. I felt for the wedding ring on his third finger, the one I had once worn around my neck on a chain while we waited for him to wake from the coma, the one I had fingered and kissed, prayed with and slipped on and off my own slimmer fingers as a nervous habit.

For a moment, before Melanie took her father's arm, I marveled that the world had kept on spinning around; all this time, through all that sorrow, the planets had kept rotating around the sun. We had healed, Bob had survived, Melanie had found love, real love again, and her girls had someone who ached to be their father.

"I want to call you Dad," little Ava had said to Dan the night before the wedding; Ava, who had barely uttered a sentence in the months after her father had died.

All of us had holes inside, I had come to understand, charred places that never really healed over completely. It wasn't possible to go through life without bruises and battle scars, and perhaps that wasn't the point anyway. Sometimes growing pains were just that—painful. But as tears rolled down my face, sideswiped by a moment of simple gratitude, I smiled as the hem of Mel's silk gown rustled by our pew and she darted her hand out to briefly touch mine.

Maybe there weren't fairy tales, or dreams didn't often really come true, but this moment felt very close. As close as it gets to perfect in an imperfect world.

Chapter 4

The Key in the Door

After I gave birth to Mack, my friend Karen gave me a valuable piece of advice from her own mother when she had her first child: "Try to get out of that nightgown by the time your husband comes home. That's going to get a little old."

I didn't seem to be able to master that one. My hair was often uncombed, my toothbrush idle in those really early weeks when everything was so upended. A shower could happen only if Mack napped or Bob was home.

I had plunged into parenting with the look of an owl blinking in the bright light. Mothering had completely recalibrated my sense of time, myself, and my body. Yet I knew from my own mother that even in the selfless early days of child rearing, no matter how much chaos had reigned during the day, it was wise to tend to the marriage. No husband, regardless of how much he loved his wife, and no wife, no matter how much she loved her husband, wanted to walk in after a long day at work and see a weepy, barf-encrusted lover still in pajamas. That image, played and replayed with each nightly turn of the key in the door, could leach love like toxins.

Bob solved the nightgown problem for me very quickly. Even before motherhood I had tended to cozy up in flannel Lanz nightgowns. Festooned with twining ivy, hearts, daisies, rosebuds, and birds trailing ribbons and bows, this had been the pajama of choice from my childhood until well after college. And each year Bob's mother had made it a tradition to give me a new gown at Christmas.

The flannel nightgowns were comfortable and girly. They spoke to lounging and cuddling and warmth. They were full-length with long sleeves and had a little ruffle of lace at the cuffs and collar and a yoke with buttons up the front. Maternal and goody-two shoed, the Lanz was exactly what you might wear to lie dreamily on your stomach and write in your diary with the little tiny key and lock. They were hands down unsexy.

One weekend shortly after Mack was born, Bob and I were sharing a glass of wine on the balcony of our one-bedroom San Francisco apartment. The sun was setting flame-red and apricot over the mountains, and the Golden Gate Bridge glowed a warm rust color. Mack was napping and I went in to take a bubble bath. We had rented a movie and were going to stay in for the night and relax.

"Honey," I called after my bath, rifling through my drawers, "have you seen my nightgown?" The sky had turned the corner toward dusk and San Francisco twinkled outside my bedroom sliding glass doors like a city of diamonds.

"As a matter of fact, I have," said Bob, and he led me out onto the balcony in my towel and pointed over the railing, his face working to conceal the mirth. He pointed three stories down onto the street, where the Lanz lay flattened and crumpled on the asphalt, marred with the tread of a dozen tire tracks.

"You did not do that!" I said, laughing. "You know, your mother gave me that!"

"Precisely," he said.

I could have put my foot down. I could have been outraged at my favorite sleepwear being turned into roadkill. But this was one of those moments in a marriage when you know you have to give. Yes, they were comfortable, but if seeing me lounging around in a Lanz flannel night-gown at the end of the day made my husband feel like I was going to warm up milk and tuck him in, well then, it was time for a wardrobe change.

I read once that romantic love, that feeling of a moth fluttering somewhere down near your groin, can be sustained for only two years, maximum. The average is more like six months. There is something so addictive about that phase of love, that sticky, sweet, languishing feeling; passion that is strong enough to convince lovers to commit murder.

But that kind of love simply isn't practical. Concentration is impossible. People don't accomplish much when they feel consumed like that.

Eventually, because humans don't seem capable of sustaining any one emotion for a long period of time, love is supposed to morph into something richer and deeper, something more realistic and functional that gets you to work punctually and pays the bills.

So for all of us in that phase of our lives right now, the question in marriage becomes How do you keep it fresh after so many years? And how do you take that pulse? I've decided that it all comes down to how you feel in that moment when you hear the car in the driveway or the scrape of the key in the door. It's what your heart does when he, or she, walks into the room.

My husband has a phrase for this, and he has used it throughout our entire marriage. He describes it as a "pang." "I still pang for you when I see you at the end of a long day," he sometimes says to me, dramatically placing his hand over his heart for emphasis. And nothing else he does will ever mean more to me.

It's a simple proclamation that we have somehow preserved the flame of that early stomach-flipping passion throughout this twenty-year journey.

With some unknowable combination of love, luck, hard work, and humor, plus a healthy dash of respect, my heart still lifts when I hear him scrabbling at the door, briefcase in hand, before bursting through to disturb the molecules of the house with his general presence and enthusiasm.

In the potential of that moment, what do you feel? I feel hope, an eagerness, relief that there are now two of us. I gear up for the final push toward dinner and look forward to the comfort and satisfaction of our heads hitting the pillow that night. Perhaps in those few moments before we drift off, we will catch up on cross sections of each other's days. With Bob home, the family feels comfortably whole. These are all the unarticulated feelings that run through my mind in one blur of color and shards of thought the moment he walks through the door.

One woman I knew of, married for forty years, made it a practice to keep a tube of lipstick right by the mirror near the front door, and when she heard the automatic garage door open, she'd run a brush through her hair and apply a slash of color. No matter what volume of baby vomit she had on her shoulder, no matter how exhausting her day with two kids, she had an image of how she wanted to present herself to her husband.

She knew he loved her no matter how her hair looked or how exhausted or overwhelmed she might be. But the lipstick, this quick touch-up, was about presentation in those initial moments of reconnection. For her, it was all about how she wanted her husband to feel when he turned the key in the door and entered their home.

A woman I know whose husband has passed away told me something once that has stayed with me. She said that if she could do it over she would not run around straightening the house and ensuring that every last spoon was in the dishwasher. Looking back through the large end of life's telescope, she wished she had spent more time just sitting in her husband's lap. It is really such a heartbreakingly simple thing to do in the end; an intimate act that connects two people in the remains of the day. Sitting entwined on the couch when the baby is asleep, finding those moments or methods, like holding hands, is the reward for reaching the finish line.

A doctor had told me once that when a person is very ill, the importance of human touch cannot be discounted. When a loved one is sick, studies have shown that their chances can improve if someone simply holds their hand. It's the human contact that raises the possibility of turning the corner.

When someone is unconscious, when family members enter the room and begin to talk, the patient's vital signs often change. When Bob was in his coma, I would put my lips to his ear and whisper repeatedly, "You are safe. I am here and I'm never leaving you. I am going to love you forever."

In those moments, the nurses showed me on the monitor, his heart rate would go down and his agitation would diminish. He would visibly relax with his family around. The doctors joked that I must have some kind of control over my husband. And I told them that perhaps he just loved me so much, all of us so much, that it would be enough to heal him. I like to think that my voice and my words were the key in the door, the answer to his awakening. And that when he felt me there, somewhere inside his injured brain, he rose to the occasion.

Of course, none of us would truly be human if we didn't also experience the opposite of these emotions—frustration, anger, and annoyance, to name a few. As much as we love our spouses, it's impossible to feel that kind of unconditional love every minute. The repetitive tasks of everyday life bring us right back to fraying tempers and the dread of sounding just like one's own mother.

After her first child was born, my friend Rene found herself at the end of her wits. She had been wholly unprepared for the one-sidedness of motherhood, and she was growing frustrated at feeling like she had to do everything. If she left her husband with the baby for merely an hour, she would return home to find a disaster. The apartment reeked, the child's diaper was saturated, and, worse, her husband didn't seem to notice. She finally complained to her mother in exasperation.

"What does he do when you *ask* him to do these things?" said her mother.

"He does them," answered Rene.

"Well, then what are you complaining about? Most men just aren't born with that device, but they can follow directions." It was simple advice, really. But that small nugget of information, that course correction, helped Rene get over the kernel of resentment that eventually sets in with asymmetrical parenting techniques and the arrival of a newborn. She no longer began to dread leaving and, even worse, returning to the apartment. She stopped getting that sinking feeling as she turned the key in the door.

I began to be aware of my own frustration and resentment as the fatigue of being a new mother set in. Like a dry-cleaning tag scratching at the back of my collar, the disparity in our parenting responsibilities became more acute over time.

I boiled over one day. "Why is it that I do absolutely everything?" I wailed, but Bob's surprised and hurt look instantly softened my approach.

"Just make me a list," he offered calmly. "The light bulbs to change, the groceries you need. Make me a list and I'll get it done at my own pace."

It was a brilliant approach that works to this day. He knows what he has to do and he gets it done on his "husband" time. And I don't have to play the nag.

Now when I go away and Bob is at the helm, I know what to expect when I turn my key in the door. I've adjusted my expectations. The kids will be fed (usually take out, with no fruits or vegetables), they will have gotten to their appointments on time (just barely), but the house will be a mess: things will no longer be in their proper places, scissors will be lost, cabinet doors open, glue sticks stuck on carpets, markers left without tops. I have come to accept all of this and understand that in my absence, with my husband in charge, my kids have been loved. Everyone will have had their father's mostly undivided attention; they will be happy and played with, and the chaos of our home won't matter. That can be easily fixed.

Nowadays, with four kids in all different directions, there is rarely time to stop in the evenings and dissect the day. Life moves ever forward, and there are so many moments that I want to freeze with Bob.

One night as we were lying in bed together I began to read something of interest to him from a novel. The cadence of my voice, the act of reading out loud to him created an incredibly simple yet powerful moment.

It reminded me of the years when we were dating, when Bob was a third-year law student and we would read and study together in his apartment. Those were the days when our hearts fluttered at the airport arrival gate, when we couldn't stop holding hands. The need to be physically connected, to constantly twine our arms around each other, was like the need to eat.

"I like it when you read to me. We should do this more often," Bob said to me.

I snuggled closer and put my head on his chest. I knew we wouldn't do this each night, maybe not even every week, considering the way he traveled and our schedules worked. But if we could do this occasionally, we might be able to touch that part of us that had existed before there were kids and a house, laundry to sort, and a pile of bills to be paid. It was one more thing to look forward to, I thought, when I heard the key in the door.

Chapter 5

The Jewelry Box

You can tell a woman's whole life story from the possessions in her jewelry box. Like reading a palm, you can trace the points where her life has intersected with memorable events, people, places, and loves. You can mark the consequential and the inconsequential, divine a sense of her self and her own self-image, spot whimsy, mistakes, milestones, and passages. You can speculate on the essence of her personality, all from what she has accumulated in that box.

The silver twisted snake ring I made at camp, the sophisticated metal charm bracelet with the Chinese fan from a fifth-grade birthday, the serious pearl earrings for college graduation, the silver bangle bracelets I wore on my right arm as a teenager coming of age, bought one summer in Vermont—I treasured all of these, although they had passed from objects of adornment into relics of the past, like a three-dimensional scrapbook.

I'd had that jewelry box for as long as I could remember. It had been purchased at a Woolworth's in Albany and had sat on my childhood dresser since my earliest memories. It was, to me, a most elegant thing: a thin veneer of navy blue leather covered the box, with some faux-Roman gold leaf pattern around the borders. On one corner the leather had ripped, revealing a flesh-colored patch, like skin, which I had once tried to color in with a marker.

A brass clasp at the front of the box made a snapping sound when I pressed the buttons on either side to open it. It had been years since I had officially shut it, and the closing mechanism hung straight out, like a tongue. The key had long ago been lost, so each time I packed to move, I wrapped a heavy rubber band around the box to make sure the contents were secure. The jewelry box was a present from my parents, although I've now forgotten why.

From the moment I had my first daughter, from the instant Cathryn was born, I'd harbored a vision of us splayed out on the floor with my jewelry box. I pictured us examining each piece I owned and my describing to her where it had come from, in great detail. I would use the jewelry to explain the stories of my life. I had saved them, in fact, for exactly this purpose.

As children, my two sisters and I had sat on the rug of my grandmother's living room, me cross-legged, my sister Meg on her stomach, legs bent back, chin in her hands. As my grandmother brought her jewelry box down to show us, my sister Nancy clapped her hands eagerly. There was treasure in that box, history and lore. Perhaps there were clues to my grandparents' marriage, the exotic places they had traveled, she a concert pianist and he a violinist, who accompanied her. Their lives had been so viscerally connected to music that in those moments when her fingers touched the piano keys and her eyes closed, it seemed to me that nothing else in the world existed for my grandmother. Not even us.

My grandmother was a mythical figure, not so much a nurturer but one who had been nurtured, like a hothouse plant. She had been raised in Magnolia, Arkansas, and had moved north to study music in college. It was there that she had met my grandfather, a "Yankee" and a musician, who couldn't have been her parents' first choice.

In her closet were fur coats and full-length dresses for concert performances. She owned multiple pairs of long white gloves, so wildly out of place in Albany, New York, and her luggage had travel stickers on its side, identifying faraway places in the Orient and Europe. The whole package was so exotic, so unusual, that my sisters and I liked to imagine her journeys around the globe and the adventures she'd had.

She loved to pronounce words in French, always drawing them out with her southern accent in a very affected way as she made us repeat them, a practice we loathed but tolerated. Her name was Margaret. No nickname. We called her Nana.

It was in the kitchen, her curling hair falling over one eye in the heat, that her southern roots really emerged. She melted sticks of butter for homemade pound cakes, put salt on watermelon, and boiled up thick okras that looked to us like soups of runny noses. She firmly believed that cooking with bacon grease was the key to mouthwatering food. There were lima beans fat as bumblebees simmered in milk, and buttery-yellow corn bread laced with ham bits. Her cooking connected us to a rich tradition of southern relatives we had only heard about in stories.

As we three sisters lay on the deep-red Oriental carpet, surely procured from some Asian jaunt, not yet into our teen years, we watched as Nana opened her large red lacquered jewelry box. Out of it she pulled ivory bracelets, ropes of beads, and Bakelite bangles. There were large brooches and rings festooned with semiprecious stones, horseshoe-shaped pins inset with tiny seed pearls, ones with leaf patterns—pieces that had been in the family for years.

As she laid the contents out on the rug, we watched the colors swirl in the Persian design and moved the items into piles, coveting the various rings and bracelets, dreaming about being old enough to wear jewelry that for now was bigger than our fists, sophisticated and otherworldly.

But the costume pieces in Nana's jewelry box were always the most fun. Jumbled all together in the box's velvet compartments, they represented the flashy flea-market side of life. They were bold colors and statements, items perhaps chosen on vacations by someone who had temporarily abdicated all of life's mundane responsibilities.

A swordfish pin called to me. Made from bugle beads and sequins and sewn on a stiff cloth, it looked like something that had been purchased in the 1940s, all glamour and whimsy, designed with a sense of humor. The swordfish's bill was long and pointy, outlined with silver thread.

"I love this pin, Nana," I said, and she winked at me as she placed it back in the box.

"Perhaps someday it will be yours," she said mysteriously. And that Christmas it showed up under the tree with a scribbled note in my grandmother's loopy, flowing handwriting.

I wore that swordfish pin the very first time I met my future in-laws. It was at a wedding in Michigan, and I was flying in to stay with Bob at his boyhood home. My roommate Nora and I had agonized over what I should wear to meet his parents. I was the "girl from New York," and I didn't want to arrive in the Midwest looking too slick. Nothing too fussy, too city, or too young. In the end I had selected a red dress in a kind of muted silk, with the giant linebacker shoulder pads that were so popular in the 1980s.

In a burst of individuality, something that would define me as a person with her own sense of self and style, I had impulsively plucked the swordfish pin from my jewelry box at the last minute. I'd pinned it jauntily at an angle on my lapel. Since then, that pin had always been a connection for me to that long-ago night, a reminder of how Bob and I had slow-danced to the band at the reception, how he had proudly introduced me to his parents, his three brothers, and his high school friends, and we'd snuck out under the club's awning to steal a kiss in the cooler air.

I had always pictured my daughter Cathryn fingering the swordfish pin, then picking up a pair of light blue aquamarine studs. "Tell me about these," I imagined Cathryn would say. And I'd remember that those earrings, from Macy's jewelry department when I turned sweet sixteen, had been the first pair of earrings my father had ever given me.

Getting my ears pierced was one of those fulcrum passages in life. It seemed, at the time, to be the single most important thing I could do to look older, more sophisticated, maybe even pretty.

While most of my friends had already gotten their ears pierced, my mother had decided that her daughters needed to wait until we were sixteen. And on this point, my mother could not be budged. It was the 1970s and hippies were changing the face of fashion, jewelry, and hair in a way that she found fundamentally jarring.

With the world shifting and revolution in the air, with rock 'n' roll, war protesters, civil rights, and busing, even in my traditional household we could sense that there was a sea change taking place out there. Respect was no longer a given, whether for elders, authority figures, or right and wrong; the old rules no longer applied. The carefully ordered white, middle-class world of the 1950s and early '60s was about to undergo a tectonic shift.

"Only ethnic people get their ears pierced," my mother said in an effort to dissuade me, and the comment makes me smile now. In my mother's eyes, real women were obviously expected to wear clip-ons. But all of the other girls in school were "putting holes in their bodies," as she referred to it. There were dangly earrings and hoops, peace signs, even the ubiquitous yellow smiley faces—plus a hundred other designs I couldn't wait to hang from my ears.

On the Saturday following my sixteenth birthday, two of my girlfriends accompanied me to the department store in my Albany suburb of Delmar, where I would join the official ranks of body piercers. Some girls used ice cubes to numb their lobes at home, then pierced them with a needle and a cork, but I was enough of my mother's daughter to be wary of this. I went to the middle-aged woman in the official-looking white lab coat standing stiffly behind the jewelry counter.

I don't remember being nervous. I was only excited. It was like some kind of ritual preceding becoming a woman, and I was willing to suffer any measure of pain for my beauty.

"How does that look?" The makeup-counter employee in the white coat peered at me over her half-glasses, her sky-blue eye shadow so close to me that I could see the creases in the lids. She had drawn two small black dots with felt pen on my earlobes and kept turning my head, using my chin as a handle, to inspect her handiwork.

"Fine," I said, too anxious to examine it carefully.

The pain was fleeting. What I remember was the look of the two small gold balls gleaming off my ears. I was certain every person I encountered could see them. Years later, after Bob slipped an engagement ring on my finger, I had the same feeling. I felt the shiny newness of the engagement band, the tiny weight of the diamonds, and I was sure that everyone noticed my hands and my ring, gleaming like a beacon.

To me, my two tiny specks of gold earrings glimmered on my body like the treasure uncovered at King Tut's tomb. They carried with them the promise that this small act would change my life. It was at home, in the fluorescent light of the bathroom mirror, that I realized with chagrin that my studs hung woefully unequally. On close inspection, one was much lower than the other. My attached earlobes—a recessive genetic trait, as I'd learned in tenth-grade biology—made the inequity even more obvious. To this day, it is the first thing I see when I put on earrings in the mirror. It's the imperfection I spot first, the lopsided inequality that no one else would ever notice unless I pointed it out.

I'd had those studs for all those years in my jewelry box. I probably hadn't worn them much after high school, but they were there. A reminder of the day that had inched me ever closer to being the young woman who would leave the nest, go on to college, and begin the next phase of the process of becoming herself.

That is why, when thieves broke into our house in Phoenix one warm, cloudless day, while we were in church, of all places, and the oleander blossoms on the back hedge were in full bloom, I lost not just my jewelry but a part of my living history.

Whoever they were, vagrants or professionals, they knew what they were doing. They entered through the kitchen window and hopped over the sink without disturbing the salt and pepper shakers on the sill. I picture them hurriedly, expertly searching the rooms for small, valuable items they could carry: a video camera containing footage of Mack learning how to ride a bike, an expensive still camera, and my jewelry box, sitting, in a naively trusting way, right on top of my dresser.

Because they had no time, I imagine, they simply took the box in its entirety, along with one pillowcase stripped from our bed, an act of utter violation that angered and repelled me for weeks. "Couldn't they have brought their own sack?" I fumed helplessly at Bob. "Don't real robbers carry sacks and wear black eye masks?"

I hated the idea that these men had touched my things, roughly opened my drawers and closets, rifled through shirts and undergarments. It was a transgression that was hard to articulate, because although I had not been touched, it made me feel dirty, angry, and victimized.

When I first discovered that the jewelry box was missing, my heart lurched. It wasn't so much that there were valuable pieces or one item I loved above all the others. It was the collective grouping of all of these bits of my life: the pewter owl necklace from my first boyfriend, ugly as sin but endearing; the outdated brooches and rings from Nana; the inexpensive chunky amethyst necklace that had so defined the 1980s as I set out to be a working girl in the big city.

I let out a little cry when I realized that the blue box was gone. There was a rectangular space of clean wood around which the dust had collected, an outline of where the box had been.

I felt naked, foolish, and momentarily angry for not having had some secret hiding place in which to stash my most beloved items, some special canister fashioned to look like a can of shaving cream or a fire extinguisher. But the truth was that all of my jewelry was valuable, even though collectively the pieces wouldn't have fetched enough at a pawnshop for a good steak dinner. Worse, they were probably lying, at that moment, in a back-alley trash can.

The swordfish pin, my little blue studs, and some of Nana's other pieces that had ended up in my jewelry box after she died were all gone. I searched desperately through the backstreets of our Phoenix neighborhood that day, hoping the thieves had picked and chosen, abandoned the bulky box in their retreat. But it was a halfhearted quest; I knew those kinds of discoveries happened only in the movies.

So the thieves had severed that connection, the one intended to pass, like a bloodline, from my grandmother to me and then to my daughter. The things Nana had passed on were now lost. The stories I had wanted to tell about my own girlish history—the pearls from my wedding, the opal necklace from a college boyfriend, the tiger's-eye ring set in silver I had made at summer camp—these had vanished. I had wanted to lay them all out on a rug with her, to watch her finger ropes of necklaces or slip bangle bracelets on her own slim wrists and choose a favorite, as I had done. But I had lost the props.

Something even more precious was stolen in Phoenix that same year. Something far more valuable than my jewelry, more priceless than the collection of all of the possessions that made up my girlhood. My ability to bear children, which had tied me to the cycles of the moon and to the sisterhood of women, would prove, in its absence, far more meaningful to me than one thousand rare gemstones or a mountain of gleaming gold coins.

After the hysterectomy at age thirty-five, which resulted from losing my third child, a son, I was instantly robbed not only of that little boy's future but my own chance to carry another child and to be a mother one more time. All at once I felt cronelike, barren, and neutered. This part of womanhood was a connection to my daughter and the other women around me I had imagined I would have until my body wound down later in life. Like the jewelry box, I had given it little day-to-day thought until it was gone. My fertility was simply one more treasure that I took for granted until I no longer had it.

What once had seemed like a monthly inconvenience now hung in my waking mind like the brightest star in the solar system. As I had hoped to do with my jewelry, I wanted to share womanhood with Cathryn, to travel the road through cramps and buying Tampax together. How would I now one day claim that tangible communal connection to my daughter?

When the nurses had first brought Cathryn to me in the hospital, I'd held her little beanlike body and touched her shock of dark hair as we fell asleep together. Gazing at her face and her satisfied eyes searching mine I put my lips to her ear. "I'm going to teach you all the secrets of being a woman," I whispered. I conjured generations of mothers passing down the holiest parts of woman wisdom almost wordlessly. I thought about the connection between mother and daughter, the infinite love and the skeins of dreams. Motherhood had given me magic powers, as if I could mystically see the pain that lay ahead for her, along with her moments of triumph, anticipation, and desire. That day in the hospital, infused with the thrill of creation, I felt sure that I would coach her to navigate her way in the world and to demand from it all that she deserved.

I did go on to be a mother again, and our twin girls were born by a surrogate after a long and interrupted journey that often circled back on itself before we got that phone call with the great news. And one day I also got a new jewelry box—nothing fancy, or too big. Over time, I replaced the stolen items with new and different ones, buying pieces gradually and sometimes in bunches. One summer I bought a dozen earrings just to make up for my loss, but I never again found the trapezoid-shaped turquoise chunks that had stood out from my ears or the silver serpentine earrings that had hung halfway to my shoulders.

And I should have known it was inevitable. By the time my own daughter reached the age of ten, she desperately wanted pierced ears, just like most of her friends. My initial pronouncement that she must be sixteen was weakening. My expectations, I was told, were out of sync with the times. Why was I so reluctant to see my daughter pierce her ears when it was all I had wanted at that age? How could I not have taken my own desires as a child and woven them into my perspective as a mother?

On some visceral maternal level, the world of piercings and tattoos, the rebellious artistic expressions of today's youth, terrified me. How had that little infant daughter with the milk-white skin transformed into this young, leggy beauty? I wanted to preserve her, wrap her in a protective cloak to keep her unmarred and pristine for as long as possible.

When I finally took Cathryn to the women's holistic clinic with the physician's assistant to pierce her ears, part of me felt as if I were righting a wrong. There would be no beauty-school dropout, no lopsided holes. I would make sure they were even, that she wasn't worried or afraid of the sting. Getting her ears pierced was such a small thing, such a minor step forward on the road to independence, but perhaps I was nervous because it was the first move.

Cathryn was anxious; when she saw the piercing gun, she asked how much it would hurt. For a split second a look of fear flashed over her face, and I thought she might change her mind. Then she squinted and asked if she could hold my hand.

When the first hole was punched, Cathryn looked as surprised and indignant as if I had pinched her unexpectedly. Before the pain could really sink in, the woman with the gun quickly and efficiently pierced the other ear, and then it was done. There was one gleaming gold stud in each ear. Cathryn held the hand mirror, pulling her hair back into a ponytail to better see each side. This small, deliberate gesture made her look older somehow, instantly more mature.

At home, I stressed that the new piercings were a privilege and a responsibility and that having them meant she was old enough to care for them herself. She needed to clean them with alcohol and she would have to put athletic tape over each earring when she played soccer, according to school rules. "You'll need to be responsible so they don't get infected," I said. "And that means cleaning up after yourself."

Two days after Cathryn's ears were pierced, one of my then four-year-olds, Nora, came stumbling down the stairs in a panic. "Claire threw up!" she screeched. "She drank some yucky water."

Instantly, I knew. As I sprang up the steps, two at a time, I understood that Cathryn had left the rubbing alcohol out and the twins, ever curious, had investigated. Sure enough, Claire was in the bathroom looking miserable and Nora began to chatter about how she had gone to take a sip herself but had known something was wrong.

"I warned you!" I turned on Cathryn with wild eyes as I dialed the number for poison control. Her carelessness could have resulted in her sister's hospitalization. It was a teaching moment and the remorse was instant; her eyes filled with tears. For one oddly triumphant, hollow second, all of my nagging, chiding, and warnings seemed to be vindicated.

We laugh about it now, the "yucky water," but Cathryn learned a double sense of responsibility that day through the simple act of piercing her ears. Not only was she in charge of herself, but her actions had consequences. She grew up more right then from what happened on the inside than the little gold studs on the outside could ever indicate.

Not long ago, I found myself on my bed with my three daughters and my jewelry box. It wasn't at all the box of treasure it had once been. I was missing the detailed history of myself prior to age thirty-four. But as I pulled out costume relics from the 1980s and '90s that had survived in a junk jewelry bathroom drawer, my girls had saucer eyes.

There was the bolero leather tie with the clasp made from a cactus postage stamp that had seemed like such a good idea on a business trip to New Mexico. I pulled out strands of big chunky fake gold chains, tarnished and heavy enough to have served as manacles. I gave my daughters my garnet beads and bracelets of green malachite from street vendors in the West Village of Manhattan. The twins oohed and aahed as I offered them the cheap cloisonné bracelets that had survived after Bob's and my first year of marriage in China.

I shed these pieces in part so that they could begin their own grown-up jewelry box, their own collection and catalog of themselves. Sooner, much sooner than I wanted to imagine, my little twins would be piercing their ears and joining the cycles of the moon and moving slowly, inexorably toward an independence that would place me in an outer circle, like one of Saturn's rings.

They would make their own choices about lovers and clothing, where to draw the line, and what jewelry to wear. Their bodies would be their own property, and with that would come decisions about tattoos and other piercings, who to let in, who to keep out. Someday soon they themselves would choose what they ate, what vitamins they took, and whether or not they wanted to be parents. And no matter what they chose, and whether or not I agreed with it, I would love them regardless and in spite of themselves.

Chapter 6

Mothers and Sons

Never having had brothers, I was always fascinated by boys. They seemed an exotic, sullen species with a curiously limited capacity to "talk about feelings" the way my sisters and I did. And they were usually dirty and disheveled.

I'd always wanted a brother, even though I knew from my friends that all they were good for was pinning you down and hawking up loogies to dangle like stalactites just inches from your face. Brothers liked to fart on your head and then run away laughing. They didn't really defend your honor or your virtue on the playground, as I had imagined in my daydreams. They would bust into bedrooms during sleepovers, stick you in cardboard boxes, and post NO GIRLS signs on their doors. Boys were always behind the garage blowing things up. Still, I felt as if I was missing something crucial.

But mothers and sons—now, that seemed like a way I could conduct some serious male bonding on my terms. I'd seen how my husband and his three brothers worshipped their mom. They lovingly teased her about heroic childhood stories in which she loomed large. They all wore goofy, cultish smiles around her, as if she had put something in their Kool-Aid long ago. Frannie was the Empress Dowager, beautiful, loving unconditionally, and ruling supreme. She elicited the kind of magnificent devotion that ultimately drove Oedipus to poke his own eyes out with his mother's brooch.

I will admit, however, that Frannie hadn't done me any favors in the housekeeping department. Her attention to every detail had left Bob a man unaccustomed to cleaning up after himself. In his bachelor pad, clothes hit the floor and stuck, dishes fermented in the sink, cupboard doors stayed open. Until I laid down the law, orange juice and milk were drunk out of the carton with one leg propping open the fridge door.

Frannie was such an ultimate mother that before her sons' dirty briefs had hit the rug, they were bleached, washed, and ironed.

Naturally, when I had my own son, I was overjoyed at the prospect of this new and wonderful relationship. Having observed my husband's filial devotion, I was excited to get a little piece of this for myself. Sons always loved their mothers, right? They had eternal, undying gratitude for the women who had brought them into the world. They would revere and protect us, put us on a pedestal and sing our praises till eternity. Eagerly I awaited the fruits of my labor.

When my son was born, I vowed I would make him the most sensitive male possible. I told myself that I would raise an enlightened being, a man who was comfortable around women, who understood them, and was thoughtful. He would be perfect.

We had dolls in the house as well as trucks, since I was determined not to guide my son into some kind of cookie-cutter testosterone toy mold. I soon realized that boys will be boys. He craved all things with wheels, as well as anything that could be smashed. And, of course, there was the universal gun phenomenon, the one all mothers have discovered, however well-intentioned or nonviolent their households are.

The gun phenomenon is simple. Rock, stick, lollipop, thumb and forefinger—it just happens. For Mack it was the banana in the high chair or the twig on the driveway. My friend Jenny's son actually bit his morning toast into the shape of a gun and began shooting. It turns out you can't mess with Mother Nature. Some things are just preordained.

Still, most of the time Mack was a sweet little boy, considerate and tender, a snuggler and a cuddler. Even so, there seemed to be a kind of man rage that existed just beneath that layer of loving. This was mysterious to me, the need to destroy things. His favorite plastic herbivore dinosaur, Sharp Tooth, would suddenly turn cannibal, a beast of the forest. Peaceful play would become warfare with the other plastic toys.

One day I stopped by the walkway to our front door to point out the workings of an anthill. I wanted to instill in my son a love of living things, an appreciation of the delicate balance of nature. We sat together and observed the army of ants moving the eggs in and out of the volcanic hole on top of the sand mound. When I got up to walk inside, he remained—fascinated, I assumed, with the order of the natural world. One beat later I heard a guttural growling noise and spun around, only to see his little light-up Power Ranger sneakers dancing maniacally on top of the anthill as he gleefully flattened it, a look of extreme satisfaction on his face.

This boy anger seemed to come out of nowhere, and I decided that this must be testosterone, a male's universal need to beat his chest. You could almost see it as it was happening, as if his tiny little gonads were acting like a self-medicating pump and a *zing* of hormones would hit right at that moment, like a cocaine addict as the first snort of crystals courses through his veins.

Sometimes this rage would present itself in the strangest places, leaving me utterly baffled. When Mack was five, we had just moved to Winnetka, Illinois, as he was entering kindergarten. I was meeting the new next-door neighbor over a thick wooden fence that separated our two yards.

She was slightly older, and I was working on putting my best foot forward, hoping I could woo her kids to become my weekend babysitters. With my three-year-old daughter on my hip, we were chatting away as Mack innocently chased down a squirrel that was scampering across the top of the fence.

All of a sudden, his raspy little voice broke the soft background hiss of the suburbs. "Get out of here, you *$#@*&ing squirrel!" he screamed at the top of his lungs, catching my neighbor in mid-sentence and silencing her like a guillotine. Even the birds screeched to a halt.

I felt my cheeks turn every possible Benjamin Moore shade of red, while a cheesy candidate's wife's smile froze on my face.

"Mack!" I admonished in what I hoped sounded like the truly shocked voice it was. "We don't talk like that!"

"Where in God's green earth did that come from?" I feebly asked the neighbor, who was looking at me slightly differently than she had been just a moment before. "Boys will be boys," she said halfheartedly, looking longingly at her back door. "I think I heard the phone ring."

Mack and I laugh about it now. He has heard the story so often that he has co-opted it as his own memory.

Over time, as all sons do, the little boy, the squirrel chaser and dinosaur fighter who would wake at dawn's first light, full of energy, became the snarling teenager, huddled and hungry for sleep in his bear cave on school mornings after a late night of instant-messaging on his laptop and listening to music on his iPod.

At first I was baffled by his plaintive cries for just another five minutes of shut-eye, which morphed into an ability to sleep till noon on weekends. The transition had been so subtle. When was it exactly that he had turned into a vampire? At what point had the kid who was always so anxious about being late for school suddenly, completely stopped caring, now timing his exit perfectly to be the last one in the car?

And how had the boy who used to devour his waffles and cereal and look forward to my homemade lunches become the kid who ate nothing in the morning and announced that he was buying lunch every day?

(In eleventh grade, heart-shaped PB&J and carrot sticks were no longer cool.)

As my son grew, and we moved to different towns, I proudly watched him through the years and into his double digits as a still-quiet boy, comfortable for the most part in his own skin. The baby rage had dimmed. At sixteen, he seemed levelheaded, he had a great sense of humor (or so others told me), and he was a good friend, a loyal friend. But lots of days that friendship didn't extend to me. Of course I didn't expect him, at that age, to crawl into bed with me after a night-mare, but I longed for a glimpse of that toddler, an unprovoked hug. Sometimes I could witness that wry sense of humor with a little smirk or a raised eyebrow and I could tell he was in there. I knew he must possess a multidimensional personality even if he didn't choose to show it in Technicolor to his father and me.

But information? I got nothing. Nada. I couldn't finagle straight an-swers on who was whose girlfriend, who was drinking, which were the bad seeds that the principal's mass e-mails hinted at. All of the real stuff, the feelings and fears, was now locked away in some kind of vault to which parents, certainly, had no access. The answers to my ques-tions were mostly monosyllabic. Was I an out-of-touch old bag? Was he worried that I would trade on information, or did he simply not have much to say? Was he lively and talkative with his friends, did he engage with his friends' mothers? That was my Achilles' heel, the worry that I'd been replaced. What if there was nothing going on inside his head be-yond sports and a need to inhale multiple carb-loaded snacks? Was he terrified that I might someday write a book?

Like all moms, I was not beneath a little reconnaissance. How else, I reasoned, would I be able to find out if I was raising a good citizen? I needed reliable sources. I knew that the network of high school moth-ers, the KGB operatives of the teenage population, could give me the scoop. And when I asked, the mothers of the girls he was friendly with and of the boys at whose houses he slept assured me he was delightful, polite, funny, and engaging.

Honestly, the only time my son truly seemed to speak was when he needed money, a ride, or my credit card to order a new pair of soccer cleats on the Internet. Okay, I wasn't stupid enough to take all of this teenage-boy angst at face value. I knew there was love there. Love took many forms. With my little seven-year-old daughters it still manifested itself in "wrap your arms around my neck and tell me you love me more than life" kisses. Even Cathryn still let me nuzzle and caress her hair. For Mack, my only son, it was not just that the bar was set lower; it was simply a whole different kind of bar.

His bar was calibrated to keep me at a respectful distance; his bar often had DO NOT DISTURB signs posted above it. And I had to rely on a different kind of mothering instinct, a more cautious, calculating approach than I used with my daughters. I was a bird-watcher, lying in wait for a rare, exotic species.

When I could get him to laugh at something I said or share a conversation about a song on the radio or how a sports team had done, I considered that a connection made.

Inside my quiet son was a mind that I knew had to be racing. At least I hoped it was racing, putting complex thoughts together and trying to make sense of the world around him, the war, the environment, the political landscape. Did he contemplate the universe the way I had as a kid, lying in a grassy field with my friend Mike and trying to figure out just how tiny a speck we were on this earth? I remembered that as a profound moment in my own childhood, feeling so grown-up and self-important, wrestling with the same questions the philosophers tackled. Did my son wonder about these things?

"Mack, what about reading *Into Thin Air* for your book report?" I offered one day when he mentioned the project. I thought the adventure, action, and suspense of the story might get his rocket boosters firing, maybe turn him into more of a reader.

"Unnggggg. . . . already read it," he grunted.

"Did you like it?" I asked, with the enthusiasm of a cheerleader.

"'S okay." So much for hoping he would read the classics.

People always said that the teen years required just being there. In some ways they were the most important time to be around and available. You never knew when teens might want to talk, might need you. So you just had to be present. But still, large tracts of it were tough going. Usually, as soon as we got in the car to drive him somewhere, Mack would immediately flick the radio on, at high volume, and the ride would become a kind of passive-aggressive tug-of-war with the controls.

When I wanted to talk I would turn the volume down. He would answer in monosyllabic grunts and turn the volume back up. Most times it was like being a driver for a mob boss: you kept your head down, didn't speak until spoken to, and went where you were told to. You were just supposed to be grateful if the folks in the back remembered your name.

But then one day, on an early morning ride to soccer practice, a glimmer of hope appeared: Mack spoke.

It started with something simple from me about how pretty it looked when the moon was out in broad daylight. Despite the anthill episode, I was still trying to pepper his world with aesthetic observations, hoping to keep that feminine, sensitive side of Mack alive. Then, all at once, Mack launched into the scientific explanation with a tone that approximated enthusiasm. They had been studying the universe in science class, and he described for me the angle of the sun from the earth and the moon. I was dumbstruck. Hadn't I been waiting for years to glimpse this kind of evolution in my son's brain?

"Do you ever wonder what is out there past the sun and moon?" I asked, trying again, in a New Age way, to open the conversation. "Do you ever think about how small our little planet is and how huge that universe is?"

I expected him to laugh or to laugh me off, but instead he continued.

"I think about that a lot," he said. "I think that there are other life-forms out there, and I wonder why we are really here sometimes. It seems so strange that there are billions of us creatures here on earth."

Mack looked contemplative and began gazing out the window. I felt proud, accomplished. This had been one of those "car conversations" the other moms all claimed to be having. The ones where their children came clean about some transgression, spilled their guts about what the other kids were up to, or asked their mother's opinion on some important issue, like girls. I felt my breast swell like a songbird's. We'd just had a real talk, something longer than four sentences.

I wanted to seize the moment, not to let this go. Clearly he was still pondering the infiniteness of the universe, our meaning in this giant, unknowable sky.

"What are you thinking about now?" I braced myself for more, feeling a bit like a cop in a made-for-TV movie who is supposed to keep the kidnapper talking until the other cops can determine his location.

Mack's head snapped toward me and a look of total satisfaction crossed his face.

"You know those little pieces of plastic on the AstroTurf?"

"Yes," I answered, beginning to feel slightly deflated. Somewhere this had taken a sharp turn, from astronomy to AstroTurf.

"I'm just wondering how many of those it takes to make a square foot on the field."

Slam. The window had come down again. Closed for business. Access to information was over for the day.

For years my son has been part of a traveling soccer team that goes to Europe each summer to play in tournaments. One July, Bob received a call saying that Mack had fallen on the field and broken his collarbone. He was being tended to in a hospital in Amsterdam. When I finally got to speak to him by phone he sounded calm and brave and even a little proud of this battle scar, but as a mother I longed to be there. Although he was taller than me and by now could easily lift me up, my maternal programming ate me alive. I needed to see my son, and he was a continent away.

Once he landed in the States we immediately took him to the doctor, who recommended surgery to screw the bone back together. Right after that operation, we all drove upstate for a vacation, six of us in the car with Mack taking up the entire third seat, propped up on pillows and high on drugs. He had been given some pretty nifty medication to take care of the pain.

It was Mack who'd insisted that we drive up that night, immediately following the operation, so he could see the friends he'd been away from all summer. The doctor had actually suggested that it might be a great time to drive, since Mack would still have some of the nerve block left in his system.

However, as we traveled farther and farther north, a moaning began in the back, then ratcheted up. The pain medications were wearing off.

Unless you are a pretty tough customer, I dare you to listen to the prolonged sounds of your child in pain. It's incredibly disconcerting to hear your flesh and blood braying like a beaten mule when there is nothing at all you can do.

Finally, after Bob dispensed the maximum allowable number of pills, I snapped. Mack was still groaning and writhing. My attempts at soothing him from the driver's seat seemed to be having little effect.

"Mack, do you know that in the Civil War the soldiers had no anesthesia? They had operations without any painkillers or even antibiotics."

"Lee," Bob began, "I'm not sure that really helps."

"They had to bite down on bullets," I continued. "Can you imagine that? The doctors just poured a little whiskey down a soldier's throat and got him drunk before they cut off a leg or an arm."

"It's not the Civil War, Mom," Mack groaned. "It's 2007 and we have painkillers." My strategy was not working.

"I think your mom is just trying to put it in perspective for you," noted Bob, shooting me a glare that said "Zip it."

More miles, more groaning. I was the one driving, and his extreme discomfort combined with my inability to climb back there and mother him was unnerving me. His pain was literally hurting me.

"Ooooooh, this hurts," he belted out, and I winced.

"Mack, just deal with it!" I snapped. "Your father has had his head blown off in a war and I went through twenty hours of labor with you before they gave me an epidural. And if you want to feel real pain, try natural childbirth—it would be like you squeezing a number 4 soccer ball out of your butt!"

Well, that was a showstopper. The car became eerily quiet. You could have heard the rack-and-pinion steering. "Life is pain," I added more quietly, as if I hadn't traumatized him enough already with the soccer-ball image.

"Wow," Bob said to me under his breath. "That was a little harsh." We didn't exactly subscribe to the pioneer "Buck it up and suck it up" philosophy of child rearing, but it hadn't escaped me that we were all in the car on a four-hour drive because Mack had demanded to head north so he could see his friends.

The twins and Cathryn hadn't said a word for some time. I glanced back toward the second seat and saw them sitting absolutely still, blinking, presumably contemplating the childbirth thing. Maybe my outburst had been a little too R for these PG viewers.

Just a week later, with his collarbone splinted in a sling, we hit our next big milestone. The piece of paper every mother both dreads and dreams of: the driving permit.

The DMV near our summer cottage in upstate New York was a small, rural office. The atmosphere was laid-back and there were people registering boats and dealing with license plate issues, with none of the long lines and stressful tones of a big-city motor vehicle department. While Mack concentrated, hunched over the paper with his fingers poking out of his sling, I worked on buttering up the lady behind the Plexiglas. I wanted things to swing in our favor, even though I was torn between joy and terror at the prospect.

As mothers, we love the idea of the license, of course, because it means we will no longer have to run out in our bathrobes at midnight when our children need a ride home. They can drive themselves to sports practice or, we fantasize, even take their siblings to a Hannah Montana concert. I would soon no longer have to broker rides with other moms or negotiate who could take my son home from soccer practice if I drove them there. Life would be easier. But there was another new emotion bubbling below the surface: panic.

As Mack took the written test, my eyes kept flitting to the notice on the wall entitled "Ten Points for Teens" (no talking on your cell phone, no drinking and driving, strict observing of the speed limit). All at once, all I could picture were the ten ways Mack's precious little head could go flying through a windshield.

Later that day, with Mack outfitted with his new permit and eager to drive, he and I headed out on some country back roads, despite his having only one good arm. Watching his profile from my spot in the passenger seat, I could still make out the boy of three or four, the one I remembered so clearly strapped into the child seat behind me. I thought back to a memorable trip when Bob and I were traveling late at night on a mountain road and I had climbed into the backseat to nurse baby Mack, urging Bob to keep going since we needed to make it home that night. It was late and there was no one on the road. I assumed, smugly, that with my seatbelt on we were safe.

Suddenly, from a stand of birches, a big buck darted in front of our small Honda, his white tufts of fur reflecting almost incandescently in the headlights. Bob maneuvered the car around him, miraculously only grazing the deer's hindquarters. The buck loped gracefully off into the woods, seemingly unhurt, but we were stunned.

How could we have been so stupid? I'd replayed that tape from time to time after that, imagining what could have happened, how awful the outcome could have been. I had kissed my sleeping son in his crib for days afterward, just reassuring myself that he was there.

And now here I was, somehow, with that grown son in the driver's seat. It was judgment day, the moment I had both anticipated and lived in fear of for sixteen years. From this point on, whenever he left the house, I would have to learn to live with the low-level hum of anxiety. Now I would no longer be privy to those little insights, those windows onto Mack's soul that came from silently chauffeuring him and his friends around town, keeping my own counsel, ears as wide open as portobello mushrooms. How had my tiny son and I moved—both in real time and at lightning speed—to this end stage toward independence?

That fall, having put the driving permit behind us in the summer, we crossed one of the last big teenage milestones. It was our very first college interview, a big one on the mommy spectrum, one that cemented for me the beginning of the end. Now he was yet one step closer to leaving our nest.

We were in Ann Arbor, at the University of Michigan, walking toward our first admissions office appointment on a Big Ten football weekend. As alumni, coeds, and frat boys spilled onto the street toward the stadium, the school's colors, blue and maize, mingled with the swirling autumn leaves.

We met up with a fresh-faced sophomore who was scheduled to take Mack on a campus tour, and I politely assumed that this was my cue to step aside. I imagined that taking your mother on a stroll through the campus and dorms was less than desirable.

"Mack, do you want me to wait for you here or inside?" I asked nonchalantly. In my head I was screaming, *Of course you want me to go with you, don't you? DON'T YOU?*

Corny as it sounds, something about the way he turned back to look at me, with a combination of an invitation and a glimmer of "Don't abandon me," made my heart turn over.

"I kind of want you to go, Mom," Mack said evenly. And I suppressed a huge urge to kick up my heels like someone who has conquered constipation in a laxative commercial.

After the tour came the interview. We found ourselves inside the hushed admissions office that quiet Saturday afternoon, when the rest of the state seemed to be at the football stadium.

I realized with a jolt that I hadn't thought to brief him. This was his very first college visit and I hadn't given him any pregame brushup, any quick overview of the proper way to behave, little pointers to remember about how to best present himself during an interview. He'd had a lifetime of my admonishment to "look them in the eye" and offer a firm handshake. I guess in some ways, by age sixteen, what's done is done, I thought glumly. If that hadn't gelled by now, maybe it wouldn't.

There we were in our first college interview ever and immediately I was talking more than I should, trying to charm the admissions person on sheer Momness alone. Mack didn't appear to be too embarrassed by me, or perhaps he was too terrified or so mortified that he couldn't even look at me. As the admissions person rolled through her introductory speech, in what was an incredibly peppy and enthusiastic voice for someone who must have had to give that spiel repeatedly, I suddenly noticed Mack's leg pumping up and down like a jackhammer.

Not good, I thought to myself, willing telepathic messages at his brain to stop all that fidgeting. Fidgeting might indicate a nervous type. Nervous types couldn't possibly be desirable undergrads, what with the giant inflow of applications she had just rattled off for the incoming freshman class.

Slowly I worked my shoe over to his foot and dug my heel into the top of his sneaker. I couldn't tell from my position what vantage point she had. I hoped I was subtle, but it was clear to me that the leg had to stop.

Next came the robotic answers to her questions. As she paused for a breath, Mack rightfully felt compelled to fill the air with a constant stream of "Uh-huh, uh-huh."

Ask a question, my brain screamed silently. *Think of an intelligent response,* I urged him in my own head, as if I were the puppet master.

Too late, I thought in despair, noticing that he wasn't making intense enough eye contact. *Look her in the eye,* I silently screamed. At the end of my stiffened arms, my hands were balled into fists.

There went the leg again, slower, like a sewing machine pedal. I slid my hand under the table and gently pressed it on top of his knee. Hard. The leg stopped. And so it went, through the hour-long session: me micromanaging and fumbling under the table to make small adjustments in his awkward, boy-body behavior. Why, now, was he slumping down, legs splayed as if he were a basketball player on the bench? Would his good manners show through? What about his posture?

At some point I must have relaxed into the interview, and I brightened visibly when Mack actually initiated a few questions at the end. *Keep it up. Sound intelligent. You're doing okay,* I thought.

On the plane trip home from Michigan, Mack replanted his iPod buds firmly in his ears and propped the SAT review book open, although I was fairly sure his eyes had glazed over. This was window dressing for my benefit. Studying for the SAT was about as interesting to him as, say, tackling a Latin grammar course on Super Bowl Sunday.

I thought about how much had changed since I'd applied to college. We were so attentive now as parents, managing every aspect of the process, signing our kids up for review courses and hiring tutors for the SAT to forensically examine strengths and weaknesses. Mothers in my community hovered over every aspect of their kids' curriculum. We had become a generation of managers driven by the fear of always needing to provide a safety net. We all stood there with our outstretched arms poised right under our children. But how would these precious ducklings fare when pushed out into the big bad world?

It was an average winter weekend and I was dropping Mack off at the SAT review course in the next town. We had picked up a friend of his, Lucy, on the way, and they established an easy banter in the car over songs on the radio. I was grateful for her female conversational skills. Mack would soon have his full license, and my spyglass view of him, these enlightened moments into his friendships and the private ways he related to others, would shrink even more.

There was something about the way he got out of the car and ambled over to her, in a caring, friendly kind of way, effortlessly holding a stack of books under his arm. He was tall, I realized at that moment—not all of sudden, the way people describe noticing a thing as if they had never noticed it before, but he was tall next to Lucy. Beside her slim frame, he was no longer a boy but a boy-man.

His walk was a bit on his toes, just like his dad's, and I was reminded instantly of how when Bob and I were dating I had fallen in love with that bounce, that joyous, ready-for-anything walk of a physically confident person. Bob had always been mostly oblivious to what the outside world thought. He expected good things from life and from all the people around him and his walk displayed that, a kind of hopefulness and comfort in his own body.

And there was something about the way Mack turned to laugh at what Lucy said, beyond my earshot, as they walked toward the school doors, that reminded me of Bob's profile. I lingered for an extra moment, transfixed by this through the car window, my eyes filling.

Something turned over in my heart and caught in my throat as I could picture, in that suspended moment, the love and care I imagined he would bestow on his future girlfriends, his wife, and, one day, his children.

I hoped that I had taught him to truly love, to lead with his heart, and to be all the things his father was to me. I hoped that I had gotten this right, fulfilled my mandate. My big job with him was done—had probably been finished for years, in fact. I could love him and advise him and throw in my two cents when it was required, but my son was already mostly himself, the man that he would someday be. All of those shoots and roots were there, inside him, already multiplying. What was left to "become" was just finish work, tinkering at the edges. The remainder would be Mack's own polishing act as his father and I stood in the wings.

But the highest honor, the greatest proof that he loves me, has been something so subtle that if I weren't looking, if I weren't ever vigilant, I would have missed. Somehow in the last few months, the boy who has been hidden in the basement in front of his Xbox more times than I'd like to admit has once again begun announcing that he is going to bed. Instead of slinking off and turning out the light as he has done for almost a year now, he has actually begun coming to find me at my computer or involved in some other household task.

"I'm going to bed, Mom, can you come up?" It's not a demand, exactly; it's not an outright request. It's just an announcement that if I'm up for it, I can swing by and sort of say good night, perhaps fluff the blanket, rub some sore soccer feet.

I call it a privilege. Soon he'll be gone, off to college, only back as a sort of regular visitor in my house. His bedroom won't be a different snapshot of disaster every day, just empty and pristine, as if I'd lost a child and created a memorial.

There are moments with him that I cherish now. Like that time, right before I wake him up, when I can get right up next to his face. I can feel the soft fuzz of his "beard," more wishful thinking on his part at this point than actual stubble. I nuzzle him, like a lioness with a cub.

He smells like a man now; his bedroom, plastered with clothes in various shades of dirty, is ripe and musky, yet he prefers the door closed. There are sock smells and sweat sports smells, all masked by certain deodorants and faint colognes. There are male smells that might wilt a plant. But down close, I can still catch a faint whiff of what used to be: that little fleshy baby smell. It's the smell of my son, the one I made, the one who loves me unconditionally, even if he doesn't always choose to say it out loud.

Chapter 7

I Feel Worse About My Knees

Most people, when they envision aging, fear wrinkles, wattles, spare tires, or—thanks to Nora Ephron—necks. Me, the terror is with my knees.

I first understood the cruelty of the knees, their ability to betray you in oh so many ways, when I was a kid. I was always that little girl buried in the overstuffed corner chair, inhaling every mystery novel I could get my hands on. One summer, an Agatha Christie novel involved Hercule Poirot searching for a murderess among a group of young girls at a summer school.

As Poirot called for a bunk inspection, the girls all lined up in neat rows. But, as youthful as her face was, the killer couldn't conceal her real age, lurking just below the hemline of the camp uniform. It was the suggestion of the slightly droopy lines, merely beginning under her knees, that indicated an older woman. She was nabbed. For them, justice had been served, but for me, barely into my double digits in age—well, I had learned to look at legs in a whole new light.

Certain celebrity magazines screamingly point out and minutely examine the flaws of starlets, drawing big red circles on the areas where plastic surgeons believe they have had work done. One month, Demi Moore's knees were the target, with before and after shots of a possible "knee lift."

It wasn't until I read that catty item about poor Demi's knees, apparently driven by her May-December romance with Ashton Kutcher, that the memory of that long-ago story and its crime-solving method came bubbling back up, like bad shellfish. The article had reminded me of one of the hard facts that, thanks to that mystery novel, had stuck with me since childhood: knees could betray you.

Let's face it: knees are ugly. They are like elbows or heels, rough utilitarian places where limbs must bend and bones connect. They are messy, like a soldered joint in a pipe. There should be lingerie for the knees, an attempt to hide the unpleasant with bows and lace.

Over the last ten years my own knees had begun to form those dreaded smiley faces, sagging underneath. If I wore boots and a skirt, where there had once been relatively smooth skin, there were now two knobs covered with something that resembled distressed pleather.

Although I'm told bare legs are in now, it may be time for me, at least, to consider stockings and Spanx. They can function like wrapping paper for the legs, holding it all in like a Jimmy Dean sausage casing. I've tried those spray-on stockings, the ones that come in a can. Spider veins, age spots—it was all just airbrushed away; but somehow the formula always seemed to rub off on my skirt and make me feel a little like Malibu Barbie. I once ruined a hotel-room rug by spraying my legs too close to the floor. I am now blacklisted at that establishment.

It's also sad that knees can disintegrate inside *and* out. Not only are my knees beginning to droop like objects in a Salvador Dalí painting, but on the inside, things are going downhill too. After years of being an intermittent runner, I'd had to retire. It had grown too painful. The bright side was, if I legitimately needed meniscus surgery, perhaps I could slip in a knee-lift at the same time. It would be similar to when people claim to have a deviated septum in order to justify a nose job.

What I keep wondering is, at what point in life did so much skin gather around the knees? When did they develop love handles? On a treadmill or the elliptical machine, I notice in the mirror that the flesh around my kneecaps moves a half beat later than the rest of the leg, like the train of a dress.

Just like with eyelids, butts, and breasts, gravity's effect on the knees is the bane of my existence. As we age, we gradually lose the connective tissue, the collagen in skin, and the muscle tone under-neath. The knee simply has less subcutaneous fat than other body parts, and the skin above the knee, on the thigh, can sag and fold over, like pizza dough when it hits the floor.

My doctor described this to me once as a balloon that has been blown up so many times that it becomes loose and wrinkly, even if you are exercising a fair amount. Eventually it is impossible for the balloon to regain its original shape. Unless we're talking about Pamela Ander-son's balloons.

Of course, even muscles begin to break down too. They can main-tain good tone well into our advanced years, but it takes an increasing amount of effort. Madonna will still look great at fifty-five, but she might need close to five hours a day to keep up those ripped arms and abs. Then again, I won't have to wear a French maid's outfit on the cover of *Vanity Fair* anytime soon, or writhe across the school carpool lane with a riding crop and stilettos.

I figure all that pursuit of perfection is too overwhelming. Do you ever just get to go out for a burger and fries? Can you occasionally give yourself permission to blow it all off and devour an entire pint of Ben & Jerry's Phish Food in front of a Lifetime movie? Perhaps that lack of dis-cipline is one reason I have saggy knees. And age spots. And wrinkles . . .

Age sneaks up on us in so many ways. I had to laugh not long ago when my husband and I were sharing a hotel bathroom. Running late, we jumped into the shower at the same time. Years ago—and even that day, I'd like to think, if time had allowed—we might have tried for a *From Here to Eternity* moment under the splashing water. Instead we found ourselves squinting and perplexed, hunched over beneath the spray as we examined the hotel toiletry bottles.

"I think this is the conditioner," I said, holding the bottle far away from my eyes and then bringing it close, trying desperately to get the small print into focus.

"No, that says body wash," he answered. "This must be the shampoo." Who knew we needed reading glasses in the shower?

So now not only am I going blind and in need of a walker for my bum knees, but I had lunch with my friend Anne, who was bemoaning her puppet lines—you know, the ones that run from your nose to the ends of your mouth and make you look like Pinocchio? I had never really thought about that part of my face before, but suddenly it was all I could see. Every time I looked in the mirror it was as if my nasolabial folds had been outlined with a Sharpie. It was as impossible to look away as when someone warns you that the person you are about to meet has a wandering eye and you try not to stare.

All of these parts of the body are busy giving out and yet hair, hair in all the wrong places, is multiplying. I'm not sure when, as a woman, I became so aware of misplaced hair as an aging issue. When, for example, did we all start obsessing about and professionally grooming all of the other hairs besides the ones on our scalp?

And when we get older, why does it begin to grow like crabgrass on a lawn in one place while in another, like the eyebrows, it begins to wisp away? My southern grandmother essentially drew on her eyebrows each day with a brown kohl pencil. She'd plucked and shaped so much during her younger years that she'd finally groomed herself right out of any brows at all. There is a practical side to this, of course. With no brows of your own, your face is a tabula rasa. Each new morning begins as a blank slate. A few quick strokes with a brow pencil and you can simply telegraph your mood for the day without opening your mouth.

Men of a certain age certainly do seem to have it worse in the brow department. Somewhere in midlife, hairs begin jutting out at all angles, like guy wires. Out they sprout, out of ears, nostrils, backs, even the tips of noses. Is there an arctic freeze coming to the planet that only men are aware of? I have to admit, all this man hair makes me dream about a completely separate bathroom from my husband's. I don't just mean a sink. I mean a whole room of my own.

Forget about coveting a polished granite kitchen countertop, a sumptuous Italian pedestal vanity, or a sunny Florida room—what I want is my own bathroom. Besides, anything that resembles a man sitting on a toilet reeks of weakness to me. Some things just need to remain a mystery.

My fantasy bathroom would have all white tiles and walls, with a giant tub and big, soft, fluffy white towels, like a Waterworks catalog. There would be white tulips, white candles, a white iPod playing the Beatles' *White Album*.

My bathroom would be a place where there were no odors, no evidence, no seats left up, and no hairs to remind me about what men do and don't do in the privacy of a privy.

Still, for all the disgust I feel when I see stray hairs on my bathroom tiles, this does *not* mean I get all aflutter at the sight of a waxed soap opera actor. I have to admit it: I prefer a guy with some chest hair. Maybe that makes me hopelessly retro, but I like a little something I can drag him around by when he gets out of line.

And yet, all of a sudden, hairlessness is the rage. Male body hair is out. It's officially totally gross. Even on the legs, I'm told. College campuses are full of young men as bare as newborn mice. University towns have sprouted waxing salons and laser offices the way they once boasted beer trucks. Now, do you have to wedge waxings in between finals? Or study for the bar while you get your back lasered?

And what happens when body nubs begin to sprout? Is it a full-body five o'clock shadow? And more important, do guys start to itch' and scratch the way we do when our bikini lines begin to grow in?

We women have understood the demands of this kind of maintenance for a very long time. We've shaved our legs and underarms, we've
plucked and primped, and in recent years we have developed new ways
to torture ourselves, shoring up "the hair down there"—our welcome
mats, if you will.

But even though we are watching, pressed to the mirror daily for
minute inspections, aging is like being vandalized by a cat burglar. You
don't know that you've been robbed until you have your own fulcrum
moment, until you look in the mirror and see that first chin hair.

"You know that one hair," my sister Meg said once. "The one that
grows back as thick as a pencil." That image stopped me in my tracks.
Then, a few months later, right after I returned from a meeting with a
client, there it was in my own mirror. It was a little, almost invisible
curling thing, like a Chinese sage's wispy white beard. Somehow it had
grown overnight, a message from my hormones warning me to buckle
my seat belt and get ready, because a goatee could be on the way.

Horrified, I thought back to the meeting. How close had I been sitting to the cute thirty-five-year-old ad executive? What were the
chances that I'd been yapping away about some serious strategic point
while everyone around the table was focused on my chin like I was one
of the Billy Goats Gruff? I staggered to my home office and sat there,
alone, my face flushed with humiliation as I replayed the meeting in
my head. Hadn't I sidled up to him at the table, throwing back my head
and laughing uproariously at his joke like a sorority girl during rush
week?

It was clear that, from this day forward, I would have to be on "chin
patrol," ever vigilant and sharpening my eagle eye for the perimeter,
like U.S. Immigration at the Mexican border. I would have to begin
stalking my own chin.

Oh, to have the body, the metabolism, the physical abandon I had
in my twenties and the knowledge and self-possession I've accumulated now that I'm in my late forties. Though isn't that just what every
old person says?

We might as well—we've all been thinking it. All of a sudden, as I and others should have been fading into respectable middle age, all around me people were cheating instead. They were getting breast implants and nose jobs, Botox and Restylane injections, liposuction that could replace good old fashioned exercise, at least for a few years, and hair highlights that instantly provided the same blond streaks I had once lain out in the sun all summer squeezing lemon juice on my hair to achieve.

Like with most things in life, I was a latecomer to the maintenance game. With a few small repairs, women around me were erasing decades from their face and figures. I had advanced into middle age, still deluding myself that all was well, living off the fumes of my supposed "late bloomer" good fortune.

My hair had stayed naturally blond into my forties, gradually dulling down into a dishwater dinge at the roots during the winter. My skin had all the carnage of the sunbathing technique that had included an aluminum-foil-covered *Frampton Comes Alive* or *The Best of Bread* record album reflecting under the chin (who didn't melt to "Baby I'm-A Want You"?) and baby oil applied directly to the face. I had those furrowed lines between my brows that I'd once thought made me look studious and focused, though I'd finally realized that they had mellowed into lines that simply made me look tired or angry, etched so deep they might grip a Bic pen vertically in their folds. I thought I was holding my own, but when I finally looked around, I saw that the joke was on me. Anyone with a checkbook or a credit card could cheat.

Though when I considered some of the frightening outcomes—the plastic surgery gone wrong, the faces that didn't move—I told myself I was all right with most of the dings and dents in my chassis.

Okay, I'll be honest: I was convinced that I would be that .02 percent of the population where something would go wrong with plastic surgery. I'd be the person whose eyelids froze during the injections, rendering them unable to blink. I'm the one who would end up with one side of my mouth drooping after someone accidentally cut a nerve during a procedure. That would be my punishment for reaching for something above my station in life.

And then I did—yes—try Botox. I was in Dallas with my husband, about to go on TV, and as I was chatting up one of the reporters, the "TV doctor" came over and began talking. The reporter (who had to be at least ten years younger than me) and I were bemoaning the lines between our brows that made us look permanently perplexed half the time.

"I'm dying to try Botox," said the reporter. And I nodded my head subtly. I wanted the results, I said, but I didn't want the process.

"Oh, it's simple," said the TV doctor, piping up with glee. "I do it all the time, and it's nothing. Just come back at eleven and I'll do you both."

Just like that. The serpent offering the apple. Now, let me just tell you that in my book, anything free is a good thing. Not only was this guy going to fix me—right here, right now, with no appointment, before I could torture myself with anticipation about it for weeks—but he was offering to do it just as casually as people shined shoes in an airport.

"Great!" chirped the reporter. "I'll be here. That's fabulous." She looked way too chipper about this.

"Okay," I said, slightly emboldened, feeling like someone at a Christie's auction who'd just raised their paddle to swat a fly.

And that was how I found myself, half an hour later, lying on a couch with a doctor I'd just met who actually had a black bag just like the one in *Little House on the Prairie.*

While most women laboriously research their physicians, Google them, rip out pages from *Town & Country*'s list of best doctors, and ask everyone they know for recommendations, here I was in a local TV station next to a vending machine, lying on a couch with gum stuck under it, about to undergo a spur-of-the-moment procedure. It was two steps away from having a baby on a Greyhound bus.

But the truly horrifying part was that the leather couch I was so casually splayed out on sat in front of a glass wall through which the entire ABC-TV station in Dallas could stare. All the directors, cameramen, and other folks swishing in and out had a full view of my impromptu outpatient procedure.

The area was a kind of employee holding tank and lunchroom, with people coming in and out for bags of Fig Newtons or nondairy creamer. As I lay there, the doctor asked me to scowl for him; then he prepared to inject the serum—a nerve poison, deadly botulinum toxin—into the two enemy lines between my brows, just inches from my brain. Now, if I eat some dicey shellfish, I'm sick for days. How is it that we have come to inject a lethal substance into our faces? I guess we all want the body "to die for."

I will kiss tarantulas, swim with sharks, cuddle snakes, but don't get me near a needle! So when I saw one coming toward my eyes, I balled up my fists and scrunched everything in: buttocks, toes, mouth, nose. My entire body was a giant Kegel exercise. And then I sucked a huge gulp of air through my teeth, kind of like Hannibal Lecter. It was not attractive, but it was better than bleating like a sheep in labor.

I'm not sure if the floor director and cameraman really understood what we were doing. Perhaps they assumed that the doctor in the latex gloves was just checking for melanomas. I'm sure folks whizzing by were unaware that some woman had just lain down in a public place to get an extreme makeover.

My husband, though, just laughed and shook his head. "This is my wife," he said unapologetically to the incredulous folks at the ABC affiliate who stopped by the couch long enough to figure out what was taking place. After eighteen years of marriage, he knew not to ever expect anything predictable with me. At least I had his sort of tacit support.

Immediately after the doctor finished the injections, it was the TV reporter's turn.

"Did it hurt?" the young woman asked me fearfully.

"Not that bad," I said, bolting toward the bathroom with an ice pack on my forehead and my eyes welling, determined to study the mirror for the residual effects.

As the doctor began injecting the reporter all around her forehead, she emitted a series of little Chihuahua yips, and all of a sudden the folks behind the studio glass were a lot more interested in what was going on. As a crowd gathered, I snuck away, just in time. While she continued yelping, the bathroom door closed silently behind me.

After close inspection under the fluorescents, I decided that not much had changed. My nerves still worked, my brow still furrowed. In between my brows it just felt a little like mushing a melting gel freezer pack with my thumb. As silly as it sounds, that day and even into the next, I felt a bit magical, somewhat ridiculous, and also a little hopeful.

When I woke up the next morning I dashed to the mirror and stood behind Bob, who was shaving.

"Do I look different?" I asked him expectantly. "Does it look better?"

Now, this is such an unfair thing to do to a husband because there really is no answer other than "Yes, dear." It is quite clear that if your wife has just lain down on a couch in front of an entire TV studio to get Botox injections, she might actually feel strongly about getting a positive reaction. She might have a little something invested in the whole process.

"You know I'd love you with your lines anyway," he said. Wise man. And I honestly believed him. But his lines made him look smarter and more mature, while mine made me look like a shrunken head.

I spent the rest of that day groping around at the grooves between my brows, half-expecting them to instantly disappear, vacillating between feeling an optimistic anticipation and guilt over having sold out my own hippie chick principles about messing with what God gave you. Botox was something approximately 50 percent of the women I knew did; nevertheless, I partially hated myself for having caved in.

Other people I knew had no internal debate when it came to tinkering at the margins with what Mother Nature had doled out. One day Holly got a set of new lips. These are big pouty lips with lots of puckering, and they stand out on her face like raw steak on a plate. I don't have the heart to ask her, but it looks as if she may have gotten the kind of implants that I imagine get laid right in each lip like those opaque sticks that go in a glue gun. Kissing Holly now might feel like pressing your mouth against the grille of a car.

And then there's my friend Amanda, who just slipped off to the doctor one day. She'd woken up one morning and felt old. Her first child had just gone to college that fall and she'd had a hard time adjusting to the rhythm of the new household, even though she still had two teenagers at home.

Without telling a soul—especially her husband, who was not a fan of "intervention"—she got some Botox injections. People started telling her that she looked great. Was it a new haircut? Was she more rested? Men, especially, couldn't quite put their fingers on it. But it was ultimately Amanda's teen daughter, the one who combs over every cosmetic product, procedure, and trend in the celebrity magazines, who called her on it.

"Your forehead isn't moving, Mother," she said suspiciously one day at breakfast. It became their little secret. Her husband didn't have a clue. To this day, he still doesn't.

And so I've decided that, like Amanda's daughter, someone can always tell. Nothing is sacred. The best approach is to just call it like it is. Don't run, don't hide, and don't pretend. There is no point in trying to deny all of the things we do in the name of looking better. Just head out there, chin up, and get your injections in front of a glass wall in a crowded TV station during the morning show.

I imagine myself with implants, how great I would look in clothes. My bras have so much contour right now, they don't even need my boobs. A big part of me thinks how wonderful it would be to pitch the Styrofoam undergarments and go back to wearing those flimsy things I bought before I became a mother and my once-firm mammaries were assaulted by pregnancy, nursing, gravity, and time.

But when I even begin to daydream a bit about buying myself a fabulous new shape, I am brought up short by something I once saw as I was biking along a beach path near the Golden Gate Bridge. A woman—she had to be sixty-five or seventy—was lying in the sun on a towel in a hot pink bikini.

She had earned her six or seven decades on the planet, and it was evident, even from a distance, that she was not a young woman, thin as she was. Her skin bore the ravages of UV rays and the mileage of a long life. But what almost threw me off my ten-speed as I whizzed by was the shape of her bikini top. Her boobs stuck straight up, defying the condition of everything else on her body. And in that moment I could picture her skeleton in the grave, ashes to ashes and dust to dust, except for those magnificent breast implants, outliving us all as they reached for the sky.

Chapter 8

Nothing with a Plug, Please

For certain women, the scariest phrase their husband can utter is "I bought you a gift." This is certainly true in my house, at least. Some husbands instinctively know how to ace that highly anticipated gift moment. Their wives receive a beautifully tailored coat or the perfect pair of gold earrings. With others, it's not limited to jewelry or luxury items. The best gifts often involve real thought. It could be a first edition book from a coveted author, a trip to the spa for some pampering, a fine custom-mixed perfume using her favorite combination of scents, or the homemade present that cannot be bought—like a sweet love note.

My husband is *fabulous*. Aren't you, honey? He still has rippling muscles, can repair anything around the house like Ty Pennington, and can scale mountains like Sir Edmund Hillary. When it comes to adventuresome, manly pursuits like scuba diving, he rivals Jacques Cousteau. His jaw is strong and his green eyes are downright dreamy.

Okay: this is the point where all of the men need to stop reading. The next part is "girls' eyes only." You guys go run off and bench-press something; I'm about to air some of our dirty little secrets.

Now that the men are out of the room, I can say it: after twenty years, my husband still flunks every test in the gift-giving category. Once we passed our china anniversary (What kind of reward is that? One more thing to wash), I might have assumed he'd have gleaned a sense of *my* style. Maybe he'd have picked up a few clues from watching me get dressed every day or seeing the kind of jewelry I purchase for myself. Again, for twenty years.

I'm not the sort of wife who sticks out her lip if her husband forgets their anniversary, or drops hints about wanting a mink coat. But here's the thing: if he is going to make the effort, pound the pavement, and spend the money, it would be nice if the end result was something I might remotely consider wearing or possibly enjoy or, if all else fails, be able to use.

But no. Recently, Bob returned from a trip; he'd been reporting in China and Cambodia. As he gathered the family around, he had a Santa-like bag.

Christmas was just a week or two away and, since he knew that I did all the shopping for that holiday, I asked him if he wanted to hold off on the gifts until then.

"Naaaah," he answered, his eyes sparkling. "I can't wait that long." I was lulled into the false hope that things might actually have changed. Maybe he had suddenly reformed, begun paying attention. Maybe, unbeknownst to me, he had been watching *Project Runway* late at night? Or, more realistically, perhaps the female producer he had been traveling with had done a little prodding and directing, like one does when training a puppy to go wee-wee on a pad.

He had some T-shirts for our son, some pajamas and an Olympics stamp collection for the twins, and then he pulled out a long slim box for Cathryn. Her eyes sparkled as she opened it: a tiny ruby-and-diamond bracelet from Cambodia. *Nice work,* I thought.

Now came the moment of drama. The wife, the mother of his children, the woman who had moved nine times during the first thirteen years of marriage because of his career . . . I could practically hear the drum roll. This had to be big.

Out of the Santa bag he pulled a small red object, a ring-sized box. Some low-level alarm bells went off when I saw the heart shape of the box, then noticed the bright red fuzzy material that covered it. But hadn't our mothers taught us all not to judge a book by its cover? After all, it was from a Third World country not known for its presentation or wrapping prowess.

All eyes in the room were on me, so I pasted that "oh so grateful expectant wife" look on my face. Popping open the box I saw . . . a ring the size of a small wheel of Laughing Cow cheese. Had I not known better, I would have thought he had purchased it for Linda Evans or Joan Collins to wear on *Dynasty*.

The stone was a love child of a turquoise and an opal. I couldn't tell what it was exactly. It looked edible. It was *big*—a giant cocktail ring, on my small, gnarled, and perpetually cuticle-frayed fingers. I'm not a manicure person, so a ring like this might look better on, say, Beyoncé or Snoop Dogg. It was clearly meant for long patrician fingers.

On one side of the stone was a spray of tiny diamonds, casually twining their way up the unidentified gemstone like ivy. And the stone was set in . . . well, what *was* it set in, exactly? The band itself was not rounded; the edges felt as if they might actually cut into my flesh.

(Later that week my friends Patti and Jane inspected the ring with a combination of curiosity and astonishment, like archaeologists on some kind of ancient dig. They came to the conclusion that the metal was almost surely stainless steel. "Look on the bright side," Patti said. "It won't rust.")

I vowed not to ask Bob what he had paid for it. Not only had he completely failed the "this is just what she'd want" test, but he'd clearly been ripped off. The only way he could have gotten his money's worth was if he had grabbed this thing out of a bubble-gum machine at the airport's duty-free stand.

"Put it on, Mom," Cathryn urged, clapping her hands in delight. This only served to magnify my inner horror.

It slid too easily over the knuckle of my biggest finger and promptly twisted around, the giant stone plummeting south like a magnet.

"We can take it tomorrow to get it sized," said Bob hopefully. I worked to keep my grateful smile level on both sides of my mouth as I rose to kiss him. "Tomorrow, or some other day," I said, still smiling.

One year, there was a necklace made of semiprecious stones and gold. It was very delicate, and I know he'd tried hard on this one, but the jewels were so pale on my white skin that my freckly age spots shone through. I can practically hear the sales pitch he must get from wily shopkeepers when he walks in scratching his head, clearly out of place and smelling of fresh meat with a ripe and supple billfold.

"Your wife will love this," I imagine a savvy salesgal cooing as she fingered the stones like a Vegas craps dealer, explaining each variety and emphasizing their value. It was a pretty, almost juvenile necklace, one that would be lovely on, say, Hannah Montana. I'm still baffled by how Bob made the connection between it and me.

Unlike some husbands, mine, luckily, never seems to notice exactly which gifts he gives are hits and which are giant stink bombs. He has sort of a UPS man's attitude toward gift giving: once he has dropped off the package, he doesn't retain a memory of what was inside. Thank goodness for that. In fact, he often appears surprised when he discovers me using one of his gifts. "Wow, I gave you that?" he'll say in a semi-astonished voice, and he'll seem to stand a few inches taller.

During my moments of introspection, I've had to face up to the fact that I'm an accessory to the crime. Part of the problem is that I'm too practical, too precise. I know exactly what I like and want, and by dictating that to him over the years, by spelling it out, maybe I've taken some of the fun out of gift giving. I can trace this trait back to my own mother, a practical, thrifty Scotswoman, well ahead of the "green" movement, who still uses her Ivory soap bits to the end and washes plastic plates and cutlery to reuse, God love her.

One famous Christmas in my childhood home, we girls sat around the tree expectantly. My father, who had this way of brandishing the big surprise gift at the end, began his customary "Well, I think there might be just one more thing . . ." in a way that caused us to squeal with excitement. After we'd opened our identical AM/FM clock radios, my father pulled out two boxes, each containing a stylish wool Geiger jacket for my mother, one red and one white. "Oh, Dave," she demurred, smiling sweetly while examining the price tags and sucking in her breath. "This is too much. I don't need two! I'm going to take one back."

My father's face fell like a hot soufflé. His hurt look gave me a little clue that this was one thing I should never do. That brief interaction was one of those backstage passes into the dynamics of my parents' marriage. I made a mental note: *Do not repeat.* But sometimes you can't fight heredity.

Two decades later, during our first months of dating, I could see the excitement on Bob's face as he handed me a big box marked with the logo of an expensive store. Inside was a long-sleeved leather minidress with a plunging neckline. Yes, that's right: a leather minidress. He was quite excited at the prospect of me stepping out in that sleek black number, looking for all the world like a Tina Turner impersonator or a *Pretty Woman* wannabe. At that moment, laying it back in the perfectly creased tissue paper, I suddenly morphed into my mother in the living room, right before his eyes.

"Oh, Bob, it's beautiful," I said. "But, you know, I really need a leather *coat.*" Bob's smile lost some wattage, and his face fell slightly. "I'd wear a coat every single day," I explained defensively. "It would get so much *use.*"

Use. Practicality was the kiss of death for a gift given out of love. But there I was, years later, making the same horrifying mistake my mother had in the name of pragmatism. And the cost for my unwillingness to let a $500 leather fantasy dress just collect dust in my closet when I could instead return it for something more *useful*? The collateral damage is that my husband no longer fully trusts his own judgment when it comes to gifts for me. At first he used to ask me what I wanted, or he'd check 'with my sisters before purchasing. Now he usually takes it at face value when I say, "Oh, you don't have to get me anything this year." Why do men ever believe that line?

So I really do have only myself to blame. But the situation has gotten so bad that it is now a family joke. When Christmas comes, if there is something I want, I just buy it. I wrap it and put it under the tree and write on the label "To Lee, Love Lee." There's a lot of chuckling and eye rolling now, and of course I always have to publicly thank myself for knowing just what I wanted. "Oh, Lee," I'll say out loud, dramatically, in front of the kids, "you shouldn't have, but I'm so glad you did!" Bob just rolls his eyes at me. Who can blame the guy for being gun-shy?

These days I don't even assume he is going to surprise me; I tell him I want a gift certificate to my favorite flower catalog so I can order some dahlia tubers. That is so unfathomably boring to him that he doesn't even act on it anymore; I just order the dahlias at some point after Christmas.

And then the practical gifts become kind of an afterthought, a sad, slow slide away from the days of courtship. There was the year he got me the espresso maker—and I don't drink espresso; he does. The next year I retaliated with the nose-hair trimmer. After all, nothing says love and romance like a nose- and ear-hair trimmer from Sharper Image. And the ironic thing? He loved it!

But I'm not alone. My girlfriends have enough horror stories to produce a reality show, or at least a healthy-sized support group. Ugly gifts seem to be a cousin to the phenomenon of bad bridesmaids' dresses, the brutal epidemic of our twenties and thirties.

When I began questioning my girlfriends about gifts, it was as if the floodgates had opened. Women were desperate to share their traumatic experiences: the huge disconnects, the insulting gifts, the too-small sizes. I began to realize that I was in very good company. I also began to feel suspicious of the wives who claimed their husbands were perfect at gift giving.

"Oh, Phillip always hits it out of the park every time," one friend cooed a bit too proudly.

"Shawn comes up with the most innovative gifts—he knows my favorite designers too," another friend confided. This sounded to me a lot like the women who try to go to their graves denying they've had plastic surgery.

"Lipo? Me? Oh no, I just went to a remote spa in Costa Rica." Or my personal favorite: "I don't know what happened," a friend told me once. "My boobs just went from an AA bra to a C cup after breast-feeding." Uh-huh.

And just when you think you've heard some of the worst gift-giving tales, another one comes along to trump all. My friend Kelly now has a rule in her house that her husband is not allowed to purchase a gift without the presence of at least one of their kids. Simply forbidden.

Her husband's first big failure was the plastic rose in a plastic vase he gave her for one birthday, early on in their relationship. And before you go jumping to conclusions: she is not allergic to flowers. But it was the plastic purse she got for her next birthday that was perhaps the lowest low. In keeping with the flower theme, the purse was molded in the shape of a watering can. Unable to bring herself to actually use it, she left it on a windowsill, as people do with watering cans, so that her husband would at least see it being displayed. Before too long the sunlight melted the glue that held the plastic seams together and the two pieces dropped to the floor.

After that Kelly's husband appears to have wised up, or maybe gotten some professional sales help, since a few years later she received a set of earrings from a nice jewelry store. While they weren't her first choice, she liked them well enough, and she wore them almost daily to show her appreciation and encourage further such purchases. On the following Christmas she eagerly opened a small box. It contained exactly the same earrings he had given her the year before. Exactly.

"You already bought these for me!" she said, pointing to the earrings she had been wearing for thirty-nine days straight. A sharp and brilliant businessman, a writer, and public-policy whiz, he, too, is missing the gift-giving gene.

When she went to exchange them, the clerk at the high-end jewelry store looked up the record. Surprised to learn that her husband had purchased the very same pair the previous year, he began to blurt this fact out, then stopped himself in mid-sentence, apparently realizing that perhaps the first pair had been for a mistress. What other possible explanation could there be? Kelly decided not to explain.

One of the great serial offenses, in my book, is giving appliances as gifts. I have one friend who has had to make a rule that her husband cannot give her anything that has a plug. No vacuum cleaners, food processors, waffle makers: those are not gifts in her book; they are work. Jill had to expand the rule to include "anything to do with the kitchen" one birthday when her husband, clearly excited, handed her a beautifully wrapped box. He stood back proudly as she opened a non-stick-pot-and-pan set. She told me that it took a great deal of composure not to hit him over the head with the frying pan, like in a cartoon.

There is also the husband who has perfected the "It's really for me" gift. This would include things like golf-ball cleaners, driving gloves, home shoe shiners, and hibachis. These men know how to top off the presentation with such enthusiasm that you don't dare point it out or act miffed. Inside, you are dying to say, "But I don't bow-hunt" or "Wow, this barbell set looks *mighty* heavy." Squashing that kind of excitement would be like attacking your toddler's Teletubbies with a box cutter or smashing a Thomas the Tank Engine toy in front of your five-year-old son's eyes. One Christmas, my friend Liz got floor seats to a Lakers game. Let's just say no one would ever choose her as a partner for the sports version of Trivial Pursuit.

And then there are the women who get golf lessons although they don't golf, haven't ever wanted to learn to golf, and don't even have time to golf. Somehow those lessons eventually transfer to the husband, who feigns outward remorse but, with a grave sense of duty, uses the certificate before it expires.

Terry's husband, Mike, spent their first dating Christmas trying to turn her into a woman from *Clan of the Cave Bear.* Doing a bait and switch, a common clueless Stone Age male technique, he innocently wrapped his gift in a beautiful Nordstrom's box, raising her hopes to a disproportionate level. Inside the box was a camping stove and a pair of high-topped waffle-sole hiking shoes.

In person, down on one knee, he asked her to go winter camping with him. Now, Terry works for a major beauty and cosmetics company. This is not a person for whom the idea of camping—even like Meryl Streep in *Out of Africa,* with porters, silverware, and outdoor platform beds—is remotely appealing. She told me that she had to open a can of whoop-ass on him after that one to bring him into line. "Do you expect me to trap my dinner, too, and roast it over the fire?" she responded when he expressed dismay at her lack of enthusiasm. Needless to say, he now camps with their kids.

But at least they made it to the *having* kids stage. For one birthday my friend Beth got a leaf blower from her boyfriend. The relationship ended shortly after that. So did that of another friend after she opened a long, thin box containing a marksman's rifle.

Lingerie, too, is something I will put firmly in the husbands' wishful "Wear this for me" category. Rare is the man who knows his wife's exact size, and rare is the woman who will love the idea of lolling around in some peekaboo see-through number from Frederick's of Hollywood. This is also an area that, without guidance, can veer quickly into Internet porn fantasyland. Anything with ostrich feathers or nipple cutouts cannot have pure intentions behind it.

Men continue to give these gifts in the never-ending desire to assume that after a day of work, making dinner, dealing with homework, and loading the dishwasher, we might want to slip on some crotchless panties and purr like a kitten. Yes, lingerie definitely falls into the "all about me" category, for everyone but the very newly wed.

Men also seem to like themes when gift giving. My friend Julie once had what she called "Christmas of the Feet," which started with a foot massager and rolled into giant, Sasquatch-sized quilted slippers. Both of these gifts failed to meet the expectations raised by their lavish foil gift wrap. Over the years, she told me, by using gentle, almost imperceptible coaching, the way a mother whale nudges its newborn calf into the open sea, she has moved him off tight-fitting lingerie and into the book and jewelry arena—a much more comfortable place to be, in her words.

The "first baby" gift is also a minefield of potential failure from the husband. Now it seems that "push rings" are expected. I'm referring to the jewelry the husband is supposed to give the wife for pushing their child out during labor. In the old days, there were no guidelines or expectations for childbirth gifts, and men were left to fend for themselves in the rewards department. This was the era when my buddy Alison got a sewing machine in recognition of the birth of her first son. If you know Alison, you will understand that the only kind of machinery she likes to operate are the things they play with on *Sex and the City*. Alison might be one of the few gals I know who would actually use a Frederick's of Hollywood charge account.

She promptly informed her husband that the last time she had sewn was when she made a pillowcase in seventh grade home economics class. She told him she would keep the sewing machine if he would lovingly wear the first suit she sewed. The next day the Singer was gone, replaced with a gorgeous fur coat, proving that some men are quick studies. He did have a relapse that next Mother's Day, purchasing three men's medium golf polo shirts for her, in gray, maroon, and hunter green—what she described as "feminine, upbeat colors."

Clueless gift giving knows no boundaries, but regifting is a completely different level. Some people regift the hideous things, the real lemons. For others, like my mother, regifting is a way to purge things that you just can't seem to throw away or that you assign a certain value to.

My mother has taken the art of regifting to a new level. Although in excellent health, for the last fifteen years she has been preparing for the end, in a long slow slide that chiefly involves getting rid of her possessions. These range from obscure gifts she got for her own wedding, such as ramekins, painted coins, or silver candy bowls, to travel souvenirs, like miniature Dutch shoes from a trip to the Netherlands on KLM.

In order to give these nonuseful items legitimacy, my mother has dubbed them "gifts from the heart." You can expect them at every holiday, birthday, and Christmas. They are my mother's version of a garage sale that goes on for years.

Among her three daughters, gifts from the heart are famous. Every Christmas we know we can count on opening a number of regifted items, from books to old tin trays she tole painted back in the 1970s, and sometimes even items one of us gave her years earlier. This past Christmas I got the citronella candles my sister gave her the prior year.

A few years ago I opened the gift of a flower-shaped candle I had bought her when I was in seventh grade. Its wax was yellowed with age. That was the same year my brother-in-law got a business-class in-flight kit from an airline that was no longer in business. We can joke with my mother about this, and she simply smiles. Old habits die hard.

Regifting is an art form. I will admit right here and now that I do regift, from time to time. I got it from my mother, like an inherited trait. I have tweaked it a bit, however; I am not shameless. I don't give things that have been opened or look shopworn. I give things I myself would like, do like, but either have a duplicate of or a similar item or just simply think I might never use. And if you believe that, I've got a used Hermès scarf to give you.

There are definite rules to regifting. Never regift an item back to the person who gave it to you. When a birthday present for my children is something I know they won't use or don't like, I'll regift it. But before I put it in the closet, I'm careful to always slap a note on it indicating who gave it. Emily Post would be proud.

Really good gift giving requires time and energy, plus a dash of creativity. I don't know if my husband can be taught. It's not that he isn't thoughtful; he is. But I think that when you are born without a nose for the perfect gift, you may simply be beyond professional help.

Ultimately, gifts aren't critically important to me. If they were, perhaps I'd make a bigger deal, assign Bob a shopping "escort," take him on a field trip to Tiffany's or Bulgari, tutor him in the halls of Bergdorf's or Barneys. In the end, cheesy as it may sound, I know he shows his love for me in other ways. I can tell you the best gift I ever got from him, and it wasn't anything I could slip on my finger or put around my neck.

It was a gift he gave me when our first two children were very young. For my birthday that year he sent me to a writers' workshop. He had researched the class and lined up the babysitting and somehow kept it all a secret. And in the end, it was gloriously, selfishly all about me.

Chapter 9

A Different Ability

"Your daughter is deaf," the doctor said, and it seemed to echo across the crowded London Clinic. It was such a final word, so frightening. After that first failed test in the pediatrician's office, we'd been through weeks of medical rigors to rule out unimaginable conditions and diseases that could be related to deafness. We'd endured months of worry, stemming from that first moment when eight-month-old Nora didn't hear the little silvery bell during what was supposed to be a routine checkup. And now here we were, living in London, and the tests were finally conclusive. *Deaf* was the word he used.

He said it in such a matter-of-fact, medical manner, as if it were just another day on the job and not my own baby daughter's life at hand. My first thought when he uttered those words was "Who will ever ask a little deaf girl to the prom?"

Somewhere in the back of my mind I had to believe that there was some procedure, an operation. Wasn't there a solution to every problem if you worked hard enough? We can now clone things, we have stem-cell research, we can fight cancer and find cures for all sorts of diseases. Surely there was some alternative therapy for this disability, some medicine that could correct my daughter's degree of deafness.

When the infant-sized hearing aids arrived in the mail a few days later, the soft ear molds, so small and pink, reminded me of the tiny cockleshells I used to find on the beaches of Florida. They were so diminutive, and what they signified so final, that I burst into tears holding them in the palm of my hand. I thought of Tiny Tim's crutch, a leg brace, an iron lung; they were the tangible artifact that would differentiate Nora from her peers.

Deaf. I rummaged through my brain and then turned to research to find solace in the accomplishments of hearing-impaired people. There was Helen Keller and her triumphant, difficult life. I called to mind the actress Marlee Matlin, whose work seemed to be mostly defined by her deafness, and I was reminded of Heather Whitestone, a Miss America winner who had beaten the odds to win. Who else did I know that was deaf? Only older people with hearing aids who struggled to catch snatches of conversations but had lived seemingly full lives. Deaf people I'd encountered spoke differently, with mushy-sounding words and mispronunciations. They used sign language. They seemed excluded, somehow on the fringe. Or was that my prejudice and ignorance?

The doctor's pronouncement felt like a huge black mark, the way evil stepmothers cursed innocent children in fairy tales. Before she had even begun living, she would have something to overcome. I would not shrink under these stereotypes society held for deaf people: dumb, mute, talk funny, gesture too much, socially clumsy. I too had held them. And now this was my daughter.

In the subsequent days, the home health visitors showed me how to fit the hearing aids into Nora's tiny ears and I began what would be one of the most frustrating periods of my daughter's hearing impairment: the "learning to keep them in" phase. I put them in, she pulled them out. I pushed them back in, she pulled them out and put them in her mouth. A one-year-old child must learn to feel that these foreign objects belonged on her body. Like a horse being broken to the bit and saddle, Nora fought this new intrusion.

As her mother, I was so vested in this process, so determined for her to succeed, that I found myself easily frustrated as we went through this exercise, seemingly a hundred times a day. Finally, it was Aura, our regular babysitter, who was my salvation. With her endless patience and deep love for Nora, she was also just one click removed from all of it. She sat in the playroom, day in and day out, simply putting the aids back in, unruffled and unflappable.

By day five, Nora had begun to keep the hearing aids in for longer stretches. She was growing accustomed to the ear molds, accustomed to what would be her "new normal."

On top of all this, I felt isolated and alone. During the intense discovery of Nora's deafness, Bob was traveling for work. Initially, he had taken Nora to a few of the appointments leading up to her diagnosis, and then he was off to China. Even though I knew it was irrational and unfair, I felt abandoned at this most important juncture of our daughter's life. But I understood the demands of his job. Journalism was not only his love; it paid the bills, too, and provided an interesting life, even though it divided us as a family at times.

We had both known the likely answer, the diagnosis, on some level, but we'd lain in bed alternately reassuring each other as we drifted off to sleep in the weeks before he left. We'd taken turns playing "the strong one," with positive statements designed to allay the other's fears.

"She's fine," my husband would say. "Did you see how she turned to us at dinner when we barely whispered her name?"

"She is babbling all the time," I'd offer the next night, halfheartedly. "She's not that far behind Claire in how verbal she is." But I knew. Some combination of doubt and worry had niggled and burrowed in me for months. Was she different? Slower? It was nothing specific, no one exact moment I could point to, and yet a mother intuits things. A mother has eyes everywhere, even deep in her own heart, and I'd known something wasn't exactly right.

After the finality of Nora's diagnosis, the more I read and learned, the harder the reality hit me. And I felt a manic need to take action, to do something as a way of working through the many skeins of my grief. I surfed the Internet. I read everything I could find, ordered books, and found a correspondence course through the John Tracy Clinic in California. I was shattered, but determined.

Processing life in the wake of Nora's "deafness," I felt trapped in my own house. I wanted to escape as much as I could, yet I knew that as her mother I had to stand and face it all. There was a weakest one in every pack. Nora was now my runt of the litter, and I needed to stand and fight for her. I thought about the many overwhelming questions: How will she talk on the phone to her friends? Will she be able to watch a movie? Listen to music or attend a concert? Will she, as a young mother, hear the whimpering of her baby in the wee hours?

I would need to defend her at times, I reasoned, to fight for special services in her education, to advocate for her like a warrior mom. In short, I would need to protect her flank until she was strong enough and old enough to do it on her own.

When it all got overwhelming, when parenting all four of them seemed too much, I would climb up to the roof of our London town house in the springtime chill. The roof was my place for a reality check when the interior of the house felt oppressive and the hearing aid rigors telescoped my vision. Sitting on the cool tar, huddled in a fleece, I would look out over the rooftops of London, the scene like one from *Mary Poppins,* with its Dickensian chimneys, and I could feel my insignificance.

It helped to get up above my life and reach for some perspective on all of it. You can't take yourself too seriously on a roof; how small my little problems seemed in the face of all that humanity, all of the people who had much bigger issues. There was a whole world out there, the endless rows of houses reminded me, a whole world of hurt and happiness, triumph and disappointment.

Watching the moon rise pale and translucent in the hours before dusk, I thought about the fact that Bob was somewhere out there, a continent away in Asia. He was working, absorbed. He didn't have to constantly live with this news like an electric hum, this exhausting reality of expectation adjustment in the forefront of his brain. He didn't have to school himself on how to articulate and repeat, to learn the baby sign language, and to shepherd Nora through hundreds of hours of therapy at home and in professional offices. I wanted to be him. I longed to trade places.

"Our daughter is not deaf!" he had said to me over the phone, broken by the slight delay of satellites and thousands of miles, and I had exploded.

"What do you know?" I had countered. "You haven't been here for the therapies, the information, the day-to-day life of keeping these aids in. What do you know?" The vehemence of my words had surprised even me, and once I'd spit them out I'd felt winded and spent. Bob was too easy a target, but I had hit the mark.

I thought of the children's story "The Little Red Hen," which I had often read to Mack and Cathryn. The hen had found a kernel of wheat, so she decided to make bread. But she needed help. She grew the wheat and cut it and ground it into flour and mixed the ingredients. At each stage, she asked the duck, dog, and cat who would help, but they all, in turn, answered, "Not I." None of the other animals wanted to help with the hard work. None of them was interested in the drudgery.

When the bread was baked, the hen asked who would eat it, and they all answered, "Oh, I will!" But the hen, who had gotten no volunteers up to this point, declined their offers to eat it and, instead, shared it with all of her baby chicks.

If Bob wanted to parachute in with his opinions about Nora without having done the hard work, without having sat, cross-legged on the floor, teary and frustrated over Nora's rejection of her new "ears," then he didn't get to have a say, I thought. He didn't get to simply eat the warm bread. What had entitled him to that?

This spiteful, childish thought felt deliciously punishing as I sat staring across the chimneys of London, beautiful in their sooty starkness against an iron-gray sky.

After a few months the genetic tests came back and we learned that the cause was a gene, a recessive gene that Bob and I both carried, although neither of us could unearth relatives who were deaf at an early age. *We have done this to her,* I thought. Our random coupling of DNA strands had combined to curse her when we chose to become parents.

Simple traits like blue eyes, dark hair, and attached earlobes seemed so benign in a tenth-grade biology book about genetics. As a parent, the manifestation of all that could go wrong when you entwined your history with another's suddenly took on a darker, more ominous tone. We had given Nora a mutation in a gene called connexin 26.

Deep in the heart of northern London, a friend guided me to Angela Harding, the director of Christopher Place. It was in Angela and her little school that I placed my hope for Nora. At first I didn't quite know what to expect, but I felt as if a building with therapists and other deaf children must be a kind of lifeline, and I worried that I had imagined Angela as an angel that would help me see some kind of light. When I finally met her she was two parts total kindness and one part get down to business. It was a rare combination and it worked, a kind of velvet fist that the kids responded to.

She ushered me into her office and we sat on the floor in the small room bursting with toys and lots of bright colors. Angela made whirring noises and animal calls and showed me how to use the toys to associate sound with objects for Nora. Nora tried to take her hearing aids out, and each time Angela patiently and efficiently put them back in. When it seemed Nora had had enough stimulation, we stopped to talk.

"Tell me a story," I asked her, choking back tears. "Tell me a story about a little girl like Nora who went to school and fell in love and got a job and had babies . . ." I trailed off. It was too painful to even think about the fact that these were only the basic dreams I had taken for granted when she was born. Now everything else was going to be gravy on top of that: the music scholarship, the grant for curing cancer, the promising political career, the brilliant art gallery debut.

I could see how carefully Angela picked her words. No one, no one seemed to be able to venture any concrete words of comfort. Deafness stands apart from other disabilities, I was told. In many ways it is one of the more difficult issues to have because the communication barriers make it more challenging for kids to truly assimilate.

"There was a little girl, it was almost eighteen years ago now," Angela began. "She reminds me a lot of Nora. She was bright and happy and she communicated already with all of the powers she had. I worked with her and her parents after the diagnosis, and I am still in touch with her. She danced and had friends and went through a rebellious phase and attended college and wrote poetry. At every stage of growing up she was first and foremost a ten-year-old girl or a sixteen-year-old girl. Wherever she was in her life she was that person first," said Angela gently, and I began to understand.

I tried to ask more questions; I wanted more accomplishment, more excelling, more tales of stupendous feats. What Angela presented me with was an average person, an average life. Nothing more and nothing less. There were no heroic role models or people curing disease or discoverers of new planets and solar systems. There were no world leaders or interpreters of ancient languages. The story she was telling me was of a girl, a normal everyday daughter, sister, girl, person.

"Did she do okay?" I asked in a small voice.

"She did do okay. Her parents grieved like you're grieving and they got on with it and gave her the best they could. They had some hard periods and some times of triumph and they rejoiced with her accomplishments and cried silently when things fell short."

"Why isn't anyone really able to give me a success story, Angela?" I asked. "Why does it all seem that no one who is deaf or hearing impaired is doing anything more than just making it? I want someone to tell me that Nora is going to be fine—that if we put in the time and energy and give her the best and if she keeps her aids in, she will be okay."

"We can't do that," said Angela gently. "No one can. Every parent wants to have a crystal ball and see into the future. Your desires aren't that much different from those of the parent of a hearing child. The thing is that none of us know your daughter yet. We don't know how much she hears exactly, how she will develop speech and language, or what kind of brainpower is in there. There are so many factors. No one can tell you Nora will be one hundred percent okay. If they do, then they are giving you false hope."

I nodded grimly through tears, realizing she was right. But I wanted more. I wanted something no one could give me. I thought about a Helen Keller quote I had read and what it might mean for Nora's future: "Blindness separates us from things, but deafness separates us from people." That sentence had reverberated in my mind as I lifted Nora out of her crib or watched her interact with her twin sister.

Later, I agreed to join a support group for parents of newly diagnosed deaf children. Not one to sit and watch people wring their hands in a group situation, I was surprised by my own enthusiasm at the prospect.

"Are you going to be okay talking about everything?" asked Nora's speech and language therapist in her reserved British way. "Will you feel comfortable sharing with a group?"

"I am an American," I responded, smiling. "We tell everyone about our gall bladder operations, our divorces, our dirty laundry. We are the land of Oprah, Jerry Springer, and Sally Jessy. You watch me, sister-woman." I laughed.

As I navigated my way to this first support group meeting, I found myself one of a motley cluster of scared, unsure parents. We seemed to be a mixture of all races and educational backgrounds. I introduced myself to a woman named Vicky, who was divorced and living in public housing. This was her third child and he was deaf. Her husband was not much help, and in denial. He had refused to come to this meeting.

Vicky was teary and shattered as she spoke to me, and we both looked at each other hungrily, like castaways on a desert island spotting a beer. I broke the ice by talking about what a carnival freak I felt like as a mother. I told her that in the past, I'd experienced the phenomenon of becoming newly aware of something and then tending to suddenly see it everywhere. "Yet when I look around me now I see no one young with hearing aids," I said to her, practically pleading. "Ever. Where are they all?"

The session leader, Zeeba, asked us to choose a partner and tell each other about ourselves. I was paired with a man named Simon, who seemed polite and well dressed. His son Jack was just six months old and his hearing aids looked so little, smaller even than Nora's against his tiny ears.

Simon talked about feeling the need to fiercely protect Jack, and as he spoke I recalled something similar Bob had said to me. It must be a man thing, I thought. My first feelings were not of protection. They were of total sadness and a laundry list of all the things I wanted her to do and be able to access in her life. It was a defeatist attitude, I realized, but at that moment in time, with that newness of discovery, it was all I could summon.

When I tucked Nora in that night, after the support group, she gave me a giant toothless grin and reached her hands out toward me from her crib, melting my heart. My world would be so much less without her. *This is not a death sentence,* I told myself. *You can do this. You can do all of this gracefully for Nora.*

My mind then turned to how I would deal practically with Nora's disability. When I was not with her, who would watch Nora when she pulled out her hearing aids and threw them down? Was the alternative not to put them in when I was gone? Who would I trust to love and care for her the way I do? Would her teachers work closely with her if she was mainstreamed? Would she be able to be mainstreamed?

After shock and grief comes anger. There were mornings, even whole days, when I felt angry at the world. I didn't need any more of life's lessons in grief or the importance of little things. I was taking nothing for granted with my new twin daughters. When people told me, in the wake of the diagnosis, to count my blessings and look at all the things I did have, I would smile outwardly. Inwardly I would think that I had earned the right to grieve for Nora's loss, while I rolled up my sleeves to get to work.

I knew that I would come out into the light again, eventually crawl out of that dark, gloomy place. Of course I was happy and grateful about all the wonderful things in my life, all four of my children and each of their gifts, but I first wanted a moment to indulge myself, to mourn the passing of my vision of my "perfect" little girl. Until I could expose and acknowledge those feelings, I would never be able to truly bury them and move forward, I reasoned.

During those weeks when I was learning to come to terms with Nora's hearing impairment, my two older children would frequently walk up to me and hug me. Mack would look deep into my eyes, as if he could make it better, or as if he were searching to divine if there was something more serious wrong, something I was hiding.

When I assured them that I was just thinking about Nora, Mack said soothingly, "But, Mom, she can hear." And I looked at him pathetically and thought how wonderful it would be to believe that the hearing aids could simply cure all of this, make it normal.

Little by little life became less painful, more its old self. The thrumming backdrop of something wrong began to recede, giving way to the routine of day-to-day life. We were all making progress. Nora, who'd been born happy and loving and patient, was thriving.

Somehow, without marking the moment, I had inched out of the blackness and toward some kind of warmer light. I was ready to celebrate both of my babies again, able to feel intense love for my family without seeing a small blight on our lives. I knew I would have bad days again, and I knew that I would jump out of my skin with joy at little accomplishments Nora would achieve that other mothers might not even notice, but my foundations felt solid again. My underpinnings were sound.

May brought nice, sunnier weather and longer days. One afternoon I took the girls to Primrose Hill Park, near our London town house. As the three of us circled slowly on the rusty whirly-turny playground equipment, a bunch of rough-looking boys who had been kicking a soccer ball on a small patch of green came thundering up. They started twirling us around really fast and I yelled out that we were going to get off, as I clutched Nora and Claire protectively.

"Are they twins?" one of the boys shouted out as he whipped us around and around.

"Yes, both girls," I said, struggling to slow down the swirling circle, which was suddenly crowded with the boys and going too fast.

"What's that on that one's ears?" one of the tougher-looking boys called out, pointing. I felt swarmed, momentarily off balance, and I realized that this was the first of many instances that Nora and I would face about her hearing aids.

"They're hearing aids," I said matter-of-factly. "They help her hear better, just like glasses help some children see better."

"Why does she have them?" loudly asked a boy with a big mop of hair.

"They let her hear things that you do."

"Why hasn't the other one got them?"

"Her hearing is fine, just like yours," I replied. I was happy with how calm I was about the whole thing, so very blasé. I was determined that Nora would feel this way about her hearing aids growing up, yet I knew it might not always be so.

On that playground I saw her as others must. The little hearing aids that I didn't necessarily notice now stuck out like sore thumbs, flopping over her ears from the motion of the little merry-go-round.

I watched the gang of boys in their public school uniforms as they ran to yet another section of the playground, my girls now forgotten. I tried to imagine Nora facing these questions each time she entered a new situation. No wonder there were deaf camps, deaf schools, deaf communities. Who wanted to feel set apart every time they went out of their home? And children could be so cruel.

Would Nora have the fortitude? Would she be able to toss off answers casually? Would Bob and I and the rest of her siblings be able to give her the confidence she'd need to stun people with her nonchalance, make them feel ridiculous for having asked?

"Why, of course they are hearing aids, silly," I imagined Nora answering, while doing something like picking a hangnail or tying her shoe. "Have you been living under a rock all your life?" And then I pictured her flashing a smile, with her killer blue eyes, and everyone would instantly wish they too could have hearing aids. She would be that cool.

Over time, in a slow evolution of months that rolled into years, Nora grew and learned and hit milestones in her speech, and I took joy in watching it all, yet a constant vigilance was required. There were therapies and more hearing aids and amplification equipment for the teachers to use in school. And we learned to speak loudly and clearly at home, narrating our actions. I often repeated myself without thinking about it.

"Why do you always say everything twice, Mommy?" Claire asked me recently.

"Do I?" I asked her absentmindedly. "Do I say everything twice?"

"See? You just did," Claire said triumphantly, as if she'd caught me red-handed. And so she had.

We spent our first summer after Nora's diagnosis back in upstate New York. She attended a morning camp and didn't lose her hearing aids once. She endeared herself to the counselors and played in the sand and napped on my lap during afternoon boat rides where the gentle rhythm of the waves lulled her to sleep.

We returned to London after summer vacation, on a clear blue September day. One week later, Nora's future and that of all the children of the world changed forever when terrorists flew airplanes into the World Trade Center, the Pentagon, and a deserted Pennsylvania field.

Two days after September 11, stunned and grieving, Europe declared a three-minute interval of silence for the victims of the terrorist attacks. As the time approached, I found myself with my friend Susan in, of all places, a British Costco, a giant imported American warehouse, the only place in England where one could purchase a forty-pack of toilet paper rolls or a gross of tinfoil.

We slowly made our way to the checkout counter, pushing a flatbed of food, drinks, and diapers, and I was sweating like a draft horse. Claire was mercifully asleep on my back, but Nora was all of a sudden wide awake and ready to get out of the front of the shopping cart.

An air horn sounded and the place immediately became so still you could have heard a tripack of double-stuffed Oreos in the back of the warehouse fall. Mothers hugged their children, coworkers sidled next to each other, heads were bowed reverently, and each person, all around Europe, became lost in their own thoughts and prayers. Everyone, that is, except Nora.

At the checkout line, people froze in mid-motion as if they were playing a massive childhood game of statues. Wriggling Nora decided just then that she would begin to cry in the confinement of my arms. So I reached for her and pulled her out of the shopping cart in an effort to quiet her. Kicking, and infused with the unstoppable need to move, she shimmied out of my arms and ran around and around, joyously turning in circles. Every time I would make a move to pick her up, Nora would let out a joyous scream and scoot away. I hadn't realized just how long three minutes of silence with a child actually could be.

Surrounded by a sea of stoic, down-turned faces, Nora thought it was some kind of game. She began to walk up to all of the perfectly still strangers around her, peering up at them with a big cheesy smile, tugging on their pant legs while screaming "Hi!" as loudly as she could. With each cheery outburst in her little girl's voice, some people smiled and others cast disapproving looks at the mother unable to control her child.

In the midst of all of that sorrow and tragedy, those brief silent moments of respectful memorial, Nora's innocent voice reminded me that life moves ever forward, even when we feel incapable of picking up our feet. People adjust, families heal, wounds scar over, although we may never forget. Nora's voice was the only noise in Costco for those three minutes, and it was as clear as a bell. In fact, it was beautiful.

Those early weeks of not knowing seem so dramatic now; all of the remote syndromes connected to deafness that the doctor had reeled off so casually that first day had never materialized. Nora passed everything with flying colors and settled into a relatively normal life. My mothering was, and still is, full of therapy and doctors appointments, audiograms and evaluations, and always staying one step ahead of what Nora might need next. I talk and talk, I articulate, I read and repeat. And this language, this rhythm is simply part of the everyday.

Looking at my nine-year-old daughter now, immersed in her third-grade life, you might not realize that she's hearing impaired. She is active, quick, and funny, she has lots of friends, she plays soccer and wears hot-pink hearing aids. She can't quite catch all the lyrics to songs on the radio, and she misses some of the things others say in a crowd. She follows people's lips with her eyes for extra insurance, and she loves giving hugs, her need for touch and feel heightened by the diminishment of another sense. Or perhaps she is just a naturally loving, demonstrative child.

Now when she pushes the hearing aid molds into her ears each morning it is just part of the routine, as mindless as brushing teeth or pulling on socks. I observe Nora as she giggles about boys, sings along to a Jonas Brothers tune, or runs down the soccer field, high-fiving her team members when she makes a goal. I marvel at her budding talents as an artist, the care she takes with coloring a picture and writing elaborate poems. Now when I think back to those early days of discovery in London, I am somewhat amused to recall my initial despair.

It was a lesson I have been shown more times than I could have imagined when I stood as a young bride, about to take the stage of the rest of my life as woman, wife, and, ultimately, mother. Back then I hadn't really understood the overarching capacity people have to adapt, to be patient, and to recover. I hadn't factored in the resilience of the human spirit, the very real healing powers of time passing, the grace and perspective we find in moments of repose, and the ability of the soul to regenerate.

In those long-ago days I saw a daughter with a disability. Now I see a beautiful, engaging person with a different ability, one that has blessed her with extra gifts and special perceptions.

Chapter 10

Take Me out of the Ball Game!

am not a sports mom. There, I said it. My name is Lee Woodruff and I am not a sports mom. Please don't judge me. I am not particularly proud of this. Surely if I were a card-carrying sports mom I'd fit in with all the other parents burning it up on the bleachers with loud hoots or huddled under umbrellas in a 28-degree sleet storm on the sidelines of the infinite numbers of games we attend.

I'm mad for my kids, and I love that they love sports. I'm proud of my children's accomplishments, and I lovingly dust all of their trophies, even if it takes the better part of a morning. But the truth is, I can't muster up the passion for the sorts of competitive combat in which other moms seem to revel.

Just so you don't think badly of me, I have tried really hard. When my son was born, I had visions of myself finally entering this mysterious and sacred territory with zeal. I imagined laying out the red-checked tablecloth on the sidelines and finally using the dusty picnic basket we got for a wedding gift, the one with the cloth napkins still rolled tightly inside. I would cheer each goal and bellow my encouragement until my voice rasped like Deep Throat's. But the reality was much more grim. The picnic basket never made it out of the basement. Spectating at soccer and baseball games for five-year-olds felt more like competing in a season-finale episode of *Survivor*.

I pretend to be interested. I jump up at the right times, taking the lead from the other parents. I holler enthusiastically. And I am genuinely excited when our team is winning, even though someone often has to inform me of each point scored and save me from unintentionally rooting for the other team. And yet, I just can't seem to make that leap to unbridled enthusiasm.

You know me. There are moms just like me sprinkled on every sideline. I am the one plopped on a blanket on the grass sneaking longing glances at the Sunday *New York Times* that has been lingering, unread, by my bed all week. The gal taking a little catnap in the May breeze. The one catching up on the week's unreturned phone calls.

This is a great time to visit with the other moms—to hear what the gang is up to, find out who is drinking, who is hooking up with whom, and harvest tips on how these women access their kid's Facebook accounts. The high school sports sidelines are the Scotland Yard of teen life.

Of course, being a sideline "chatterer" has its penalties. I may be deep in conversation when a goal goes in. "Warning!" one of my friends will say. "Cath got a goal with an assist from Maddy." This way, when Cathryn asks me the inevitable question in the car—"Did you see the goal?"—I can answer, "That was an amazing assist from Maddy. You guys work well as a team." No harm, no foul.

I never played team sports. I tried cheerleading once, but it wasn't really for me. I couldn't do the splits, didn't fill out the letter sweater, but I did like the pom-poms. Perhaps some of my reticence had to do with my fear that the human-triangle part of the routine might collapse, with me on top. Whatever the real reason, I quit after the first season.

There are more explanations for my lack of interest in sports. I only had sisters. Title IX wasn't in full force until I was in high school. My dad never followed sports, and our family never had a favorite team. We didn't gather around the TV to watch the Super Bowl.

I can definitely trace some of my aversion to sports mania back to one particularly painful moment in middle school gym class, smack-dab in the vortex of the formative years.

There we all were in our antique navy blue gym uniforms with front snaps and elastic at the legs, looking like something out of the Edwardian lawn tennis era.

"Hey, Lee," one of the cool girls casually yelled across the locker room. "Did you see the Jets game last night?"

As I unsnapped the gym suit and got ready to grab my towel, I paused. The popular girls were including me; they were asking me a question, as if I were in the club. And I really did want to be in the club, if only for a moment.

"Yeah," I answered, lying through my teeth. "Yeah, I did." I can only imagine how hopeful my eyes looked then. I was a lamb to the slaughter, grateful for this crumb of acceptance as they stood there all naked and bosomy, snapping their bras on around their waists, while I caved in my own chest to hide my mosquito-bite breasts.

Before I even had a moment to feel partially accepted, one of the crueler girls spun around and fixed me with a beguiling smile. "Well, that's funny," she spit out, "'cause there wasn't a game on last night!" *Whompf.* Complete humiliation.

My son and husband are quick to highlight my lack of knowledge in this arena. They like to belittle me with what they call the sports test—they both rattle off team names and I have to call out the sport and city. I'd say I'm up to about fifty-fifty right now, after years of drilling. I should probably try to improve, if only to wipe the smug smiles off their faces.

My husband comes from a family of four boys. All they did was play sports. Football, lacrosse, soccer, and ski racing on weekends, with everyone piling into the family station wagon to head to northern Michigan.

Bob's mom, Frannie, recounts legendary tales of driving them from one field to another, while they changed uniforms in the back of the station wagon. I picture her in those years, crisscrossing the Detroit suburbs to and from their various games, a look of beatific satisfaction shining on her profile as the varsity lacrosse or Pop Warner football teams tackled their way to victory in the setting midwestern sun.

The reams of uniforms covered with dried blood and grass stains, the gear and equipment, the smells and the body odor; she embraced it all with vigor. I'm quite certain she never thought to complain once. She was the ultimate sports mom. This is definitely *not* the sort of woman Bob married.

I'm operating on the slim hope that Bob's intensity for the kids' games takes me off the hook a little bit, gives me some license to slack off. After all, if we have one sports-crazed parent, isn't it better for me to balance it out with a healthy dose of apathy? If Bob were a total opera nut or passionate about, say, hooking rugs or crocheting pot holders, maybe I'd need to make more of an effort in the sports department. But he's not. He's a sports fanatic. And that's why the kids' sports education falls squarely on his shoulders. I regard this as a simple division of labor. I mean, this is a man who designated a "sports father" for his son, a role with the same guiding principles as those for a godfather. Bob's fraternity brother Jed received the honor of this newly minted sports education role, in case anything happened to dad during Mack's formative years.

We had an unspoken deal when we started our life together that Bob would be the guy in the yard throwing the ball and playing catch. He'd be the one drilling our kids on their footwork and their stick handling. As the mom, I'd lean more toward the Cookie Monster–shaped cake for birthdays, the Candyland and Clue marathons, and the homemade Christmas wreath and over-the-top nativity scenes in our living room. It's a little traditional, a little old-fashioned, but I've always felt that parenting was about optimizing our skill sets.

My sister Meg told me once that her husband, an avid skier, had felt complete and total satisfaction once his kids had become accomplished at the sport.

"I can die now," Mark said to her one night on a ski vacation after a long day on the mountain. "They've done all I wanted them to do."

"But what about being nice people and good citizens?" she asked him playfully. "What about intellectual curiosity?"

"Nope," he answered. "You can cover those bases. This was my big dream as a dad."

Perhaps Bob isn't that much of a zealot, but at times he's come darned close. When Mack was five, he was playing on a little tykes' soccer team in Phoenix. Mack, like most of the boys his age, found the bugs and the grass at his feet far more interesting than where the ball was on the field.

Bob was close to despair. "My son is going to stink at sports," he moaned to me on the sidelines, holding his head in his hands like a cartoon character. "Look at him—he isn't even interested in the ball." Mack slipped both hands down the front of his shorts to scratch his crotch. It did appear somewhat hopeless.

"Bob, he's only five," I pointed out. Bob still looked glum.

In any case, soccer was better than the alternative. As far as I'm concerned, Little League baseball was invented to test a mother's love. Watching Mack's team of eight-year-olds one hot Saturday, I was reminded of Chinese water torture. *Drip, drip, drip*—none of these poor kids could hit the ball. *Drip, drip, drip*—no one ever seemed to get to bat. *Drip, drip, drip*—some little kid in the outfield just sat down and began pulling the grass up by the roots. Okay, okay, I know this sounds un-American, but I remain truly suspicious of the Little League mother who can stay focused for nine interminable innings of what mostly amounts to groin scratching and a solo workout for the catcher.

Somehow, though, my husband would sit there rapt through each inning, as if Mickey Mantle himself were at bat. I would wait for what felt like a month of Saturdays until my precious son finally came up to the plate. In the outfield, it would have taken the efforts of three nuns saying novenas for him to catch the ball or for it to fall anywhere near him. No one was more grateful than me when he moved on to soccer. At least in that game there is constant movement, even if, in the early days, Mack remained rooted to the ground.

Some sports are simply more fun to watch than others. I was excited when Cathryn made the JV lacrosse team. But at the first game I realized the school subscribed to a "Kumbaya" approach. Anyone who wanted to play could join the team, so the ranks were swollen to the size of a small telephone book. This meant that Cath didn't get on the field that often. This also meant that I could get through the giant stack of catalogs and coupons that got shoved through the mail slot daily.

"Mom, I saw you reading magazines during the game," she accused me one day as we headed to the car after victory.

"You weren't playing at the time," I answered lamely. "Were you?" She rolled her eyes in answer. We were smack-dab in the middle of the eye-rolling stage of life.

"Don't you like watching me?" she said, and the scalpel of guilt nicked my heart. Girls can be masters of manipulation.

"What if I was really, really into quilting bees and I made you come to them every week?" I asked my daughter. She stared back, unappreciative of my humor.

"Mom," she said, exasperated, "you're the mom—you are supposed to come to my games, like all the other moms. And you're supposed to watch," she added.

I have to admit that for all of my failures, I am getting better. Like someone in a 12-step program for nonsports parents, I've been taking baby steps. I'm actually having a lot more fun, too. And when my little David Beckhams score a goal? I can feel the elation and the pride. When they miss, the agony of defeat.

It took me a few years, but I now actually remember to ask who won. You're chuckling, but that question wasn't always the first thing that occurred to me when they walked in the door. I was the mom who asked if they "had fun." I know, I know.

I'm still working hard to channel my inner fan. I'm actually a pretty enthusiastic yeller on the sidelines these days. But even then something goes wrong. During one game this past season I was inwardly proud of my cheerleading on the sidelines. After a while, though, I noticed that the other parents seemed subdued, downright quiet in comparison to me. It wasn't until halfway through the first quarter that one of the other moms gently broke it to me that this was "Silent Sunday," the one day during soccer season when parents on the sidelines were not allowed to open their mouths.

All at once, the furtive looks Cathryn had shot me while running down the field made sense. She was mortified. Silent Sunday had supposedly been designed to teach us all respect. The idea was to let the kids figure it out on the field without the coaches and parents screaming directions and kicking the sideline dirt in disgust.

Honestly? I think it was created to teach all of those loud and mean parents a lesson—you know, the ones in the folding chairs with the school team colors and logo emblazoned on them, the ones with two PROUD PARENT OF AN HONOR STUDENT bumper stickers on their minivans. These are the folks who yell things at the referee you wouldn't consider uttering in a normal social setting, things you might only say to a pedophile or a repeat offender.

I saw one mother, sweet as a southern sorority sister with a sweater set and pearls. Her hair had been blown out as perfectly as Christie Brinkley's. Judging by her looks, you'd expect her to jump up on the toes of her Tory Burch flats and clap her hands in delight when her child scored, while serving cucumber finger sandwiches to the other parents at halftime.

But when this little flower opened her mouth, what came out was the equivalent of the Bronx cheer. "Ref, what kind of a bull——t call was that?" she screamed in a voice that might have shattered glass in the breakfront down the street. Silent Sunday was developed to give us a reprieve from people like her.

You want to know my real triumph? The area where I really shine? Snack mom. That's right. When it's my turn to supply the drinks and snacks, I am in my element. I start preparing a week in advance, being sure to include a healthy fruit along with something somewhat sinful, like cookies or gummy worms. Of course, half of the battle is presentation. The juice boxes are perfectly chilled in the cooler, the orange slices are cut just so, and the Oreos gleam in the sun on my plaid moisture-wicking sports blanket.

For one, brief shining moment, my brilliance on the soccer sidelines shines through.

Chapter 11

Swimming Through It

Nobody can see me cry when I'm in the water. Through the disappointments, losses, and sorrows of my life, I have always swum. Swimming surrounds me in the velvet wet of a bluish-green world where I can dive deep down and sob with no trace; it gives me a secret place where I can grieve. For me, the water is a primal and embryonic balm, life in its most elemental form.

Anytime I want to simply escape life's gravitational pull, I dive under and open my eyes at the bottom of a pool, pond, or lake and make the world go away. Swimming is my own indulgence, my chance to turn inward and feel connected to another element, the comforting quilt of the water. Sunlight refracts off the windows of the natatorium, the air, the top of the water, turning it into shards of aquamarine, blue, turquoise, and green like sea glass. When I'm encased in water, the world underneath is all mine, an invitation for one.

The act of swimming, slicing through the water with rhythmic strokes, has always made me feel embraced, ensconced, and protected. In college, when I learned that my grandfather had died, I went swimming. I went to the water to be comforted by my own simple movements, so I could remember him and cry. That was when I learned how the pool could mask my tears, and that was why, years later, when Bob was gravely injured, I returned to the water to grieve.

I've been swimming since I was a tiny child. Like a flock of geese, our family has returned to the same small town on northern Lake George every summer for five generations. That connection to the lake is almost chemical. It is an opiate, a balm. The loamy moss scent near the shore, the gentle sound of waves lapping on the rocks near the boathouse, the shocking plunge make me feel closer to the elements.

My parents ensured that we had proper instruction in anything to do with water safety. Each year at the local Silver Bay camp my sisters and I earned YMCA badges with names like Polliwog, Minnow, and Flying Fish. There were boating and canoe courses, sailing lessons from my dad, and practice on how to dock a motorboat. But all of this was unimportant, in the grown-ups' eyes, unless you could make it to shore in an emergency. Being proficient, saving yourself, was part of living near the water.

And so swimming became second nature for me at an early age. As a girl, I created my own ritual of swimming to the pine tree at the point across our bay. It was simply a part of my day, and I loved the peace I felt far out from shore, the way I would find pockets of warm and then cold, the sight of spindly tree trunks on the bottom of the shallower parts of the bay or a fish's nest, long ago abandoned. I dreamed about what treasures the bottom held: money and old cans, the silver ring from my first summer boyfriend that had slipped off and twirled slowly to the sandy bottom while I was learning to water-ski.

It was all for fun and relaxation until one day, when I was a teenager, I was diagnosed with scoliosis, a curvature of the spine. This officially thrust me into the world of swimmers.

"You're going to need to do regular exercises or you'll end up having surgery and wearing a back brace," the drill sergeant orthopedist barked at me after the examination. He was trying to scare me into action. He knew teens were lazy and unmotivated, that they didn't stick to routines. To drive his point home, he arranged it so that our second visit would occur at the children's hospital, on the ward where kids with back problems were recovering in scary traction contraptions and casts. I pictured it: me in a back brace at the junior prom, me in a bikini over a full body cast at the beach for graduation? I embraced his exercises with gusto.

"If you're smart, you'll take up swimming," the doctor said. He was the team doctor for the Buffalo Bills and he was gruff and tough; when he spoke it sounded like he was chewing gravel. I didn't like him at all, but I was determined to prove to him that I would win. I'd never be one of those poor kids in a hospital bed if I could help it.

"The crawl is the best way to build up and strengthen your back muscles without putting weight on them," he told me, adding, matter-of-factly, "Find a pool." Easy for him to say. Getting access to a swimming pool wasn't a simple thing in our new town of East Aurora, New York, at the time. This is not a convenient sport.

But inconvenience hasn't been enough to stop me. Once I entered the working world I became a morning swimmer. I joined the ranks of the odd, somewhat obsessive-compulsive subculture of humans who rise between five and six A.M. Like zombies, we trudge in all types of weather to a communal pool, don unforgiving skintight Speedos, and freestyle our way from end to end like fish caught in a tank.

For more than twenty-five years now, morning swimming has given me a jolt. My best days have always started with me rising early and heading off to swim. Living in cities like London, San Francisco, and Washington, I could walk to the pool hauling my duffel bag full of the tools of my trade: extra suits, shampoo, lotions, and goggles. I have a comb and conditioner, a latex cap to hold back my hair, a knit hat for cooler mornings. In other cities we inhabited—Richmond, the outskirts of Chicago—the car ride was part of the journey, as it is again now, in the suburbs of New York.

Waking before dawn I dress in the dark, fighting the urge, especially in the dead of winter, to snuggle back under the warm blankets. After tugging on my suit and then sweats, I pull on my boots and jacket, start the car engine, and watch my breath make puffy dragon clouds as I work the ice scraper against the car's frozen windshield. I relish the special jump I have on the day. The rest of the neighborhood is dark and quiet, except for the occasional light in a bathroom window or the solitary reflector-clad runner I pass on the short drive to the YMCA.

The warmth and simple utility of the locker room, the chlorine smells, and the cold tile in the shower are all familiar now. As I enter the pool area a rush of warm, humid air greets me, and I test the water first with my toes before jumping completely in and springing off from the pool deck.

We morning swimmers are an odd lot. That kind of commitment draws seriously type A folk. Through the years I've swum with accountants and teachers, public servants and students, mothers and investment bankers; swimming draws people from all walks of life. And yet there is an easy camaraderie, a familiarity that develops among those who inhabit the locker room at that hour. Wary of outsiders and short-timers, morning swimmers line up like ponies at a gate, jostling for the lanes, anticipating the payoff, that first break of the water's surface.

I slip into a new skin just easing into the water. The very act of meditating through movement rearranges the molecules in my mind and body for the half hour or forty minutes that I do laps. The rhythm of swimming becomes a chant, and I relax into it.

My precious block of time in the water lets me organize my day. There, in the swimming pool, no one can press their demands on me. As I swim, I create my own reverie, a no-fly zone for the outside world. Swim, touch the wall, turn around, swim back, touch the wall.

I get some of my best work done in the water. I write lead sentences, find solutions, create comprehensive to-do lists, and use mnemonic tricks to remember them. I am thoughtful in the water. I remember relatives' birthdays and notes I need to write. I compose e-mails out of the blue to check in with distant friends. And I daydream. I play out fantastic dramas behind the curtains of my mind. I've met fabulous people and accomplished noteworthy things. I've had beautiful lovers and been friends with movie stars and musicians. I've won Oscars, walked on the moon, and driven a race car, pulling off my helmet to shake out my hair at the finish line.

Returning home, I push the button on the coffeemaker and the day ahead seems to crackle with possibilities. I know that this feeling will be gone by nine that evening, replaced with the fatigue of a long, full, multitasked day. But while warming my hands around the first mug of coffee, I feel a sense of accomplishment before anyone else in my house is even awake. The stillness of the bedrooms upstairs, my four children's soft sleeping breaths, the anticipation of the day in my peaceful kitchen—these are my rewards for rising early.

In the morning, braced to face the frenetic school routine, I relish my post swimming glow. The addictive feeling of vitality and strength, of lengthened muscles, makes me stand taller. And the sense of completion allows me to feel more whole, as if I've just finished planting tulip bulbs in the fall or cleaning out a closet.

"Swimming is so boring," the uninitiated say to me. Repetitive, yes, but never boring.

In aerobics class, or even yoga, my teacher chants and calls out the various positions, demanding total focus on what the body is doing. You concentrate on your breath, on your muscles; you concentrate on concentrating on letting go. The goal is to push back all stray thoughts, to apply discipline to the mind. Even running, a sport I enjoyed until my knees gave out, requires a kind of mental background vigilance: for the occasional careless driver, an uneven sidewalk, a large stone or tree root obscured on the path.

I've tried to find other satisfying types of exercise, but they've never stuck. Especially when the kids were young and Bob was out of town, I'd do what I could to exercise at home. There's an expensive treadmill and an exercise bike in my basement. It would be so easy to drift down there in the mornings and never leave the comfort of my warm house. But I simply can't muster the interest. It all feels so confining, so penned in.

Being a swimmer carries its own identifying traits. For one, you always smell like chlorine. It permeates your hair and your skin, leaving a faint whiff that I don't even notice anymore. But, still, I've wondered, didn't they kill people with chlorine gas in World War I? I've long nursed a secret fear that one day, after my lifelong love affair with the sport, they will determine that swimming in pools is dangerous for your health. The chlorine is certainly strong enough to change my hair color. Once I began highlighting my hair, the powerful chemicals in the water actually gave me punkish lime-green streaks, until I bought a special shampoo that removed it.

"You've been swimming," my kids will exclaim when I nuzzle them, and I suppose that will be the smell they remember me by. Scents are visceral. I recall my grandmother's Shalimar perfume, my dad's English Leather cologne, and the vaguely musty mothball aroma of our lake cottage when we first opened it up in early summer. A smell can instantly take me back to a place or a person, like the faint peppermint odor of my grandfather's wool shirts, or the rich waxy scent of the red lipstick my mother applies daily. My children, for better or worse, will most likely remember the smell of chlorine.

If my husband ever worries that swimming is only an alibi, that instead I am entangled in a lover's bed in an illicit affair, he only has to smell me. He tells me there is something oddly comforting now about the faint whiff of chlorine on my skin, after all these years.

The morning trip to the pool had become a rhythm in my New York suburban life, a pattern that abruptly ceased the day Bob got hurt. In Bethesda Naval Hospital, caring for him, I found myself existing on adrenaline, scared and anxious. I needed to swim. It alone, of all of my activities, reminded me of what had been normal, natural, even mindless.

When I walked back into the Bethesda–Chevy Chase YMCA for

the first time that horrible winter, during a cold snap that, after the swim, would freeze my wet hair, the core group of those same morning swimmers from when we'd lived there in the year 2000 was present. My friend Margaret didn't crowd me, or rush up to hug me and, with an overly sympathetic expression, ask a million questions about Bob.

"We thought you might come," she said simply. "We hoped you would come." And she thrust toward me a bag containing a suit, a swim cap, and goggles. She'd bought it when she'd heard Bob was injured and coming to Bethesda. She had been keeping it in her car, she explained, waiting for me. These were the basics, the swimmers' stock-in-trade, and she'd been hauling that bag into the locker room hopefully, every day, waiting for me to return to the fold.

This simple gesture touched me in ways I can't easily articulate. Although I'd never played organized sports, I imagined this was like that, the feeling of being part of a greater whole. This communal caretaking among the sorority of locker room swimmers was the closest I'd come to being on a team. And it felt like coming home.

For one hour in my crazy ICU-centric day, swimming allowed me to perform a simple, mindless, repetitive activity. I wanted my brain to cease its jarring patterns, to stop fearfully spinning like a tire with no traction. I wanted to stroke through silky water, one arm over my head and then the next, arcing out and striking the surface with my hands. I wanted to slice, to cut, to throw myself into the liquid calm of the water, hoping for a tonic. And I could cry; cry in a way that I was unable to in the ICU, in front of the doctors or my sisters, Bob's parents or at his bedside. For all of them I needed to remain strong and hopeful. I needed to shield them from my constant fear that he might never recover or talk again, that he might not recognize me or even love me. The water was like a leach field into which I could pour all of my sorrow as I stroked through each lap.

I swam throughout the weeks Bob was in his coma, rising for the day at 4:30 A.M. I swam, I prayed, I chanted and daydreamed, I pretended that my family inhabited an alternate life, the one we'd have if we'd never left D.C. At the YMCA I could make believe I was there on any ordinary morning, ready to go back home and pack school lunches. And eventually, it worked. Bob woke up and began the slow path to healing, and life became chaotic again in a different way.

Through the years and through my pregnancies, the act of swimming was a blessed relief from the gravity that moored my feet to the ground. As my belly grew, the feeling of weightlessness was a salve to my aching back. There was a part of me that hoped to imprint my passion for moving through the water on my unborn babies. Maybe they would learn to love swimming by osmosis. It would be one of my gifts to them.

So I was incredibly worried when I was pregnant with our first child and we learned that my water had broken in the pool. One afternoon at home, almost a week past my son's due date, I began to feel a slow leak that seemed out of place. It was subtle, not the giant splash that I'd always heard described.

When I got to the hospital, the tests revealed that almost all of my amniotic fluid was gone. The baby could be in distress, so they'd need to induce labor. It was when I recounted my past twelve hours for the doctor that she surmised my membranes must have ruptured unnoticed while swimming. There was too little fluid left for it to have been a slow leak.

Of course, as a first-time mother I was terrified that swimming had perhaps injured the baby; the air had gotten in, the chlorine had done damage, I had opened my child up to infection. I worried and worried until they put Mack in my arms and laid him on my chest. Then I knew I would make him a water baby. I would teach him to love to swim.

Each summer since then, returning to our lake, my children have watched me kick off from the dock in the afternoon to take my usual swim to the point. It's the one time each summer day when I can leave everything behind on the shore. Once I'd secured my young ones under the watchful eye of a sister or my mother, I'd begin the twenty-minute round-trip toward the pine tree, touch the slippery rock, and head back, savoring a simpler time from my girlhood where this was the one responsibility I had to myself all day.

There is always a moment, in the center of the bay, when I stop, roll over onto my back, and just float in the blue-green womb of the lake waters. I marvel at the sapphire sky, the puffiness of a cloud, or the way the mountains roll down, deep and dark pine green, to meet the shore. I began this ritual as a teenager, and as a young adult the moment of calm became a welcome reflection, silent as a prayer, for whatever excruciating life forces were buffeting me.

Now, as a mother of four, lying still in the middle of the lake is pure meditation. No matter what chaos has ruled the day in our family, a moment on my back looking at the sky immediately puts it all in perspective. When I was once asked to come up with an image that would calm me or put me back to sleep, it was this one: me, on my back, in the center of our bay.

One bright August afternoon, a few years ago, Cathryn sidled up to me on the dock and announced that she wanted to accompany me on my swim. I unenthusiastically envisioned a slow crawl next to a dog-paddling daughter who would ultimately tire and then complain, sure she'd never make it. She was the child who could whine eternally about a splinter and overdramatized the distance to the raft. I agreed, on the condition that her father follow us in the kayak, just in case she couldn't finish.

As the second child, sandwiched between her brother and twin sisters, Cathryn is often neither the first nor the last. She is still looking to define her place in the family, and while she is the oldest girl and the big sister, she usually concedes most "firsts" to her brother. She is strong and confident in ways I don't think I embodied at her age, and under her sometimes-wimpy feigned exterior, she has a mostly can-do attitude. She isn't a quitter in general, and she certainly wasn't on this swim. With each stroke, as her confidence grew, I began to understand that she was going to do this for herself and for me. She was going to make it across the bay.

After a while I went on ahead, then turned back, and began to swim toward her, suddenly panicking that I was missing this, that I hadn't been thinking about her journey for what it was. It was her "first," something her big brother had not yet attempted to do. As I swam closer her head looked like a small frog in the water. There was no stroking now, just an obvious motion forward, driven at this point by sheer will. "She hasn't stopped yet, hasn't even touched the boat," my husband called out proudly. I swam up beside her and she broke into a huge smile. I could see that she was tired. But I was so proud, and told her so.

"I've never been out this far, Mom," she huffed between froggie kicks.

"And you are swimming so well," I urged in a soothing tone. "Look at the distance you've come and how little is left."

"It looks like a lot," she said, her voice wavering.

"I'm going to teach you my special trick," I cooed. "Turn onto your back and look at the sky." She looked at me questioningly for a moment, and then we both rolled over and gazed up. "Take a deep breath and just stare at the clouds," I said. "Whenever I want to relax I just swim out here and float like this in the middle of the lake, and it makes me feel better every time."

I looked over at her thin body, her face still clenched in determination. She was concentrating on seeing what I saw, focusing on the landscape and the sky. We picked out a cloud that was puffing up into the shape of a chubby sheep and caught the tops of the mountains out of the corners of our eyes. As her mother I know that she will never see exactly what I see. She will find her own shapes in life and view the landscape through her own prism. But I can help her find her place in that world. As we lay on our backs, toes touching, I urged her to feel the sensation of surrendering to weightlessness and serenity, the joy of lying still, ensconced in water.

Chapter 12

Money Can't Buy Me Style

When I was in a Texas airport the other day, a woman made an odd gesture to me from across the departure lounge, slapping her rump like a bronco-busting cowgirl. As I waved and yippee-yi-yayed my way back to my seat, mimicking her friendly gesture, I felt my boarding pass and ID poking slightly out of my new J. Crew corduroys. I waved again and, after a few minutes of gesturing, the fun was over.

"Thanks," I called to her, tucking my license back into my pocket and giving her a confident thumbs-up. She smiled back weakly. *What a nice person,* I thought, and I went in search of a magazine.

It wasn't until later that night, passing by a full-length mirror in my hotel room, that I realized what she had been trying to tell me. There—stitched across my entire back pocket—was a large Kleenex-sized piece of linen, a label I had somehow failed to see. Stamped on the linen was my size, a giant red number with an S next to it, to indicate the length. Not S for small, as in Kate Moss, but S for short, as in stumpy.

Yes, I'd been parading around, going to the bathroom, buying snacks, perhaps genially fielding what I thought were friendly smiles and smiling back. I had been the butt of everyone's joke. Literally.

There are women who seem to have been born looking put together, and there are women who walk around with tags stapled to their rumps. There are gals who can wear a full face of makeup while pumping out miles on the treadmill at the gym, and then there are those, like myself, who end up with raccoon eyes even just applying mascara. I envy the iconic women who were the early adopters of leg warmers in the 1980s, or the rebirth of the poncho in the late '90s. They were also the first to buy heels with pointed toes—roach killers, really—while I was sure it was a one-season fad and that rounded or square-toed shoes would be in forever.

I have friends who accessorize to perfection. Their shoes always match their purse, which matches their lipstick shade, which matches their sunroom curtains. I wear whatever I pick up off the floor. I'm definitely guilty of the "top of the drawer" dressing philosophy, too. If it's been put back clean on top of the other shirts in my drawer, it gets worn over and over. You can see the pattern developing. Wear it, wash it, put it back, and then pull it out again. There are clothes in my dresser I haven't even seen in eight years.

My friend Suzie showed up at elementary school pickup the other day all decked out in patent leather high-heeled boots and a floral dress I'd just seen in *Glamour*. "You look great," I said. "Where are you going?"

"Oh, nowhere," she responded breezily. "I just wanted to wear a dress today."

The few times I've shown up with makeup on at kid pickup, my friends have asked me if I had a job interview.

I am happy with a pair of khakis and a Target T-shirt. I can understand why women in those polygamist cults gravitate toward the same one-colored, long, mutton-sleeved dresses. It's effortless.

Thankfully, my "mom" uniform is more comfortable than the businesslike gray suits I purchased just out of college. Perhaps you recall the craze in the 1980s for working women to look as much like buttoned-up Wall Street bankers as they could. There I was in a gray blazer and skirt, a little red silk bow tie at my neck, and nude stockings. With sneakers.

The suit was of thick wool, and as my mother had taught me, I had put all of my winter items away for the summer with mothballs, to be sure to protect them for next year. The idea of new seasonal clothes was foreign to my upbringing. As I put on the gray suit one morning, I got lightheaded from the aroma of mothballs, but I assumed that it would fade in the open air.

Only it was raining. And when the rain hit the wool, all hell broke loose with whatever life-threatening chemical is in a mothball. As I rode the elevator up to the top floor of my office skyscraper, everyone around me parted like the Red Sea, noses crinkled in distaste as if I had let out some unmentionable gas in the confined space. I was a pariah. Worse, I had to spend the day in that outfit—stripped down to the skirt and shirt—until I could get home and throw it at the dry cleaners. My whole office was infested with the scent. I smelled worse than a flooded basement.

I once wore a skirt for an entire day without realizing that the back flap was completely stitched up. I wondered why I had to take mincing geisha steps, until I eventually saw the big X sewn across the pleat in the back. So much for looking elegant. I'd also just assumed that all women's jackets had nonworking pockets.

When I was in college, a fraternity boy told a friend of mine that she didn't "dress to attract men." The comment was meant to be constructive, but it hit a nerve with her. This was the era in which we East Coast college women wore baggy clothes. It was a preppy period, the

Reagan years, dominated by polo shirts and the worn L. L. Bean look, sort of a precursor to shabby chic. None of us was completely comfortable in our own skin, obsessed as we each were, in those tumultuous years, with our weight and body image. All of my roommates, myself included, had our own particular vices: we rationed tiny boxes of Sun-Maid raisins, we used laxatives, we ate whole pizzas drunk and then ran miles to burn it all off.

"You don't dress to attract men." I've often thought about that phrase, as it describes me too. I was never one for body-hugging clothes or things that might show off my figure a little too much. I've always been more *Leave It to Beaver* than *Sex and the City*, more Mary Ann than Ginger.

Once, at a black-tie event in Manhattan with my husband, I was seated next to a famously rakish male celebrity while wearing a turquoise designer dress that was a tad more revealing than my style, but beautifully cut. It had been picked out for me by a friend. As we talked politely about life and my kids, he scanned my wardrobe.

"Are you from New Jersey?" he asked me, his eyes flitting over the bodice; I'd been pulling the plunging décolletage back together over my woefully inadequate cleavage all night. I suddenly went from masquerading as a fashionable gal-about-town to Carmela Soprano.

When it was time for our family to move to the New York area after two years in London, I knew that my comfortable mommy wardrobe, complete with baby-spittle stains, was going to need some updating. I was going back to work as a PR person for Benefit Cosmetics after a hiatus. I'd be heading into Manhattan regularly from our suburban home to meet with sophisticated and stylish magazine beauty editors. When I touched on the topic of clothes with some of my friends, I got an earful.

"First thing," said one. "Lose the stirrup pants."

"I don't wear stirrup pants and haven't since those eighties Whitesnake videos," I retorted defensively. Was that it? Was that their image of me? A throwback from the 1980s MTV era? But she'd hit on something. My sense of style was a season or two behind the times. Okay, maybe seven seasons.

I preferred to buy things on sale, which usually meant they were the previous year's goods or one size off. (That's a euphemism for ill-fitting.) Even though I was now a mother myself, I had never given up the philosophy my mother had taught me: always buy a size or two up to "grow into." Last year, I eagerly pulled a green-and-white-striped balloon-hem sundress off the sale rack in late August. When I finally wore it to go out to dinner that fall, I looked like a Victorian bather. The slicing glances of other women in the restaurant led me to believe that I should go back to the turn-of-the-century sanatorium and get my lungs checked for consumption.

"You have to look 'city' when you go in for these meetings," said Betsy. "Not ten-year-old Talbot's blouses and yoke-patterned cardigans." She knew me. I'd tended to gravitate toward pale colors, until finally someone told me they washed me out. I had once been advised that I was a "spring" on that old '80s Color Me Beautiful wheel, and I'd embraced those palettes earnestly, being drawn toward the flowery pinks and lavenders, soft mint and baby blue the way an old, incontinent dog finds its way back home after being dumped two neighborhoods away.

"You're talking to fashion magazine editors," said my friend Sherrie. "You are going to have to give up the sensible-shoe thing."

"But I really can't walk in heels," I sputtered. "I don't know how women do it. The foot isn't supposed to fit into a triangle. Didn't Chairman Mao ban this in the countryside?"

"Black," said my friend Cheryl. "It doesn't really matter what you have on in New York as long as it's black. You can get away with everything."

And so I did. I bought lots and lots of black. Over the next few years I would have enough black in my closet to be a regular at funerals in Sicily. And somewhere along the way, just when I had stockpiled a closetful, blue became the new black. And then gray.

No matter how I tried to get it right, I still looked mostly wrong: the wrong shoes, some of my younger sister Nancy's hand-me-downs. The fact that she was giving them away should have been my first clue. I couldn't bear to part with certain clothes that I knew I'd paid a lot for, or hadn't yet worn. (Like the white raw silk skintight pants with the now too high waist that I'd been saving for several seasons, hoping they'd come back in style.)

But in the recesses of my closet, I was still secretly violating the one code that my friend Carol had told me was taboo in most American cities.

"Absolutely no holiday sweaters," she'd said. "Under any circumstances." Keeping my face neutral, I'd thought back to my closet, which at one point in time, not so long ago, did harbor a Halloween sweater and still most definitely had a Christmas sweater. Okay, both were still in there—but hang on before you judge me. First, there had been a kind of suburban sweater mania back in the early '90s. Second, this Christmas sweater was really more of a black shirt with buttons on the front. Stitched into subtle squares were fir trees and maybe a Santa head or two. Both of these sweaters had been gifts from my mother-in-law.

The Halloween sweater, which had been popular when we lived in Richmond, along with the holiday flags people put out on their front-porch flagpoles, was somewhere toward the back, I was almost sure. It had been a gift during the days when sweaters were big and baggy and worn over leggings, and on a cold day it was rather comforting, the way walking around your house in a Patagonia sleeping bag might be. Its ghosts, pumpkins, and witches dwarfed me. When I moved down the grocery-store aisles, I must have looked like a self-contained walking kindergarten parade. I knew I would need to find the evidence and remove it from my closet immediately, before anyone discovered it. On the other hand, what if holiday sweaters came back? . . . Anybody with me?

I once found a barbecue-themed sweater vest in size XXL at a country store in Vermont and promptly bought it for my friend Kerri. It had spatulas on it and bottles of ketchup and mustard, there were over-sized wieners and even a few green dill pickles floating on the navy background. As themed clothing goes, it was the jackpot. For a while that vest went back and forth between us, kind of the way people pass around fruitcakes or gag gifts among a group of friends during the holidays. The point here is that I did know my limits. I did understand the difference between hokey and marginally acceptable. Or I thought I did. But now, returning to work part-time in Manhattan as a forty-something, all of what I'd known about the image I presented to the world was coming into question. I'd need to look pretty sharp to convince these much younger, much hipper magazine editors that I knew my moisturizer from my primer. In the end, it was clear that even the Christmas "shirt" would have to go.

Over the next few years, as I worked for Benefit Cosmetics, I pretty much pulled it together on the clothing front. But little things were still amiss. I still wore sneakers and carried my heels in my backpack, right up to the minute before the meeting. And I guess that the fact that I liked to carry a backpack, a vestige from my college and diaper bag days, probably said it all. When I should have worn tights or stockings, I often cheated with knee-highs, as I hated that twisted-crotch feeling of nylons.

So then, last year, it happened again. Another clothing intervention. "You know, we have to deal with your clothes," said my good friend Elena. The occasion was my upcoming book tour; I was about to go on the road and be in front of the media for the book *In an Instant*, which Bob and I had written. Clearly she had some grave concerns. I was not offended, though I thought I'd done okay since moving to the New York area. Obviously I was still not ready for prime time. "We need to get you some professional help," Elena said. And she did.

Weeks later, I found myself in Barneys with Laura, an amazing clothing wizard. She quickly began pulling out suits and dresses for TV and speaking engagements, pretty little cocktail ditties for fancier occasions.

"You really have a cute figure," mused Laura, examining me like a painting, hands on hips, as I stood on a wooden box in front of a three-fold mirror. "You need to show it off more."

"I can't breathe," I said as I tried to wriggle out of a silky black number that was holding my ribs in like a whalebone corset. "Are you sure I shouldn't go up a size?"

"NO!" said Laura and Elena in unison, rolling their eyes at each other. I was hopeless.

But Holy Mother of Gandhi! The price of these items would have fed a Nicaraguan family of five for months, maybe years if they eschewed some proteins. I was accustomed to bargain hunting. When we lived in Phoenix, a store aptly named Last Chance had ruined me forever for retail. That one store had been the dumping ground for Nordstrom's items everywhere, the unsold, the returned, and the damaged. It was a treasure trove of great stuff if you knew how to hunt or were willing to get the zipper on a fabulous pair of designer jeans repaired or sew a button on a blazer. It was hard to think about paying full price for anything after I'd cut my teeth on those aisles.

"Wow," I said, feeling faint as I checked and double-checked the price tag. I wiped the tiny beads of moisture from my upper lip and tried to understand how one little unlined dress could cost the same as airfare to Cambodia.

"Think of it as an investment, Lee," said Elena evenly. "You just have to. You want to be taken seriously." She was as cool as a cuke.

And so began my Eliza Doolittle stage of becoming glamorous. I tried hard to meet the vision of what I was expected to be, to keep my high heels on my feet and wear waist-revealing tops. Like a kid with multiplication tables, I memorized which separates went with which, unable to create my own combinations. And during my fifteen minutes of fame, my goal was simple: try to look chic and pulled together. It was a low bar.

Bob's and my very first public appearance as a couple after his injury was to pretape the *Oprah Winfrey Show*. Everyone asked me if I was nervous, but I didn't feel it. I imagined Oprah to be just as she was: kind, concerned, and someone to whom you could probably tell your deepest secrets. She was everyone's girlfriend. I felt like it was just the three of us chatting. As Bob and I sat on her couch, my legs crossed in a pair of jet-black stiletto-heeled boots with side zippers, my feet felt like they were into S&M.

"Great boots," Oprah said at the commercial break.

"Macy's, ninety-nine bucks on sale," I yapped, trying to understand why, for some annoying reason, I was always quick to point out a bargain to everyone, as if I weren't deserving of owning full-price merchandise. Oprah laughed. Sort of.

I'd also purchased a nice set of fake diamond studs, fairly hefty rocks, before the book tour. I'd been complimented on the "beautiful earrings" a number of times.

"Oh, they're totally fake," I would always confide to the women who eyed them admiringly.

"Can't you just simply say thanks once or twice?" my stylish friend Julie asked me. But I didn't feel comfortable being the kind of woman who either demanded or accepted four-carat earrings on each lobe. Inside, I was still the practical gal who would trade in real jewels to pay the utility bill for the coming decade.

An old adage says that you'd better put on good underwear every day in case a bus hits you and they have to cut your clothes off in the ambulance. The new saying in our family is that you'd better have a nice outfit on when you head out because you never know when you might just meet the president. This is exactly what happened in 2006 when we made the worst-dressed list at the White House.

We had scheduled a White House tour to keep the children busy and their minds off their dad's grave injuries. President Bush and his entourage were somewhere in the Midwest at a fund-raising dinner.

We'd been spending a lot of time at the house of our friends the

Bakers in Washington, and they had come on the tour with us. They have three perfectly beautiful and lovely blond girls. And each was turned out appropriately for the White House tour in a kilt skirt and navy cardigan, hair pulled back in a ponytail with a bow and a headband. They all but sang "Edelweiss" on the steps of the West Wing.

All at once we got word that the president was arriving home earlier than expected. Would we like to go out and watch the helicopter land?

So, on a freezing winter night, we found ourselves on the White House lawn with my twins and Lizzie Baker swinging on the stanchions, just as the Secret Service had explicitly forbidden.

Nora, completely unimpressed with her surroundings, had already asked me twenty-five times throughout the tour if she could eat her White House M&M'S, complete with George Bush's signature on the box. Forget that the box itself was a collector's item—Nora couldn't wait to rip it open to get at the candy. "Go ahead," I finally said. Since not one of us had brought a warm jacket, maybe the intense sugar injection would warm them up, I reasoned.

All at once the press corps seemed to change positions. A set of small lights appeared in the dark sky, like bright shooting stars over the Washington Monument. Two were decoy helicopters and one was the real McCoy, with Bush and his staff inside.

The first chopper swooped in and then abruptly peeled away. The other two approached and then one took a sharp turn with the well-lit monument in the background. The third helicopter glided over the rolling White House lawn and hovered for a moment before proceeding to land in slow motion, as if defying gravity.

With the copter just dozens of feet away, our hair began blowing wildly as the blades swept up the wind. Next to me our adorable blond White House tour guide was texting madly on her BlackBerry. As the helicopter touched down she laid a hand on my elbow, yelling to be heard over the rotor blades.

"The President would like to ask you if your family can wait a few moments more," the guide told me. "He would very much like to meet with you in the Diplomatic Reception Room." A small ripple went around our group like a game of telephone as all ten of us gathered together in the chaos and noise of the moment.

Once the president was out of the helicopter and had declined comments, but waved merrily to the press, our guide began to thread us around the cameras and over the TV cables. We were ushered into the first room under the awning, right off the lawn, blinking from the sudden brightness of the lights and the warmth of the room.

I was the last one in, like a mother hen at the end of the brood. I tried to collect myself. What would I say? I knew that Bob's injury had been just the randomness of war and horrible timing, but it was hard not to think that if the war hadn't happened, my husband would be safe and sound instead of lying comatose a few miles away in an ICU, with an uncertain fate. I tried to knock the thought out of my head as I entered the warmly glowing White House room.

I stuck out my hand and looked President Bush right in the eyes. His face was much kinder and warmer than it appeared in pictures. His eyes were moist, and he trained all of his attention on me.

"How are you, ma'am," he said genuinely, and he squeezed my hand. "I am so sorry for what has happened to your husband. How is he?"

"He is doing great, Mr. President," I answered. "He's a fighter and he is hanging in there."

"How are the kids doing?" he asked, looking at the sea of mostly girls and clearly trying to figure out which four were Bob's and mine.

They swarmed around. Mine looked like extras from *The Grapes of Wrath*. You know the scene where they're traveling across the dust bowl during the Depression? The helicopter wind had whipped the twins' already gnarly hair into a natty Don King special. When was the last time I had actually washed their hair? I had relied on the hotel pool as a bathtub. Nora's mouth was rimmed with chocolate from the M&M'S. My kids' Walmart sneakers had one side that lighted up and one that didn't. They were wearing cheap sweatpants outfits, purchased at the tip of Long Island, which was why the slogan "The bitter end" appeared on the butt. All that was missing were the toothpicks, so we could enter the room cleaning our teeth and picking the dirt out of our fingernails. That surely would have completed the picture.

Barney and Miss Beazley, the president's two black Scottish terriers, had been let into the Diplomatic Room and were putting my girls over the top with excitement. Nora and Claire began jumping up and down at the sight of the dogs, looking like two escapees from an orphanage.

And then the younger girls suddenly broke the moment and turned it all into a spontaneous giant hugging session. Nora and Lizzie simply ran up to the president to hug him. Claire ran toward the dogs and then the president. I may have visibly cringed as he began patting Claire's four-day-old chlorine-stiffened rats' nest.

We all posed for one last shot and the president moved in next to me while the camera clicked away. "Again, I am so sorry for what you all are going through and what happened," he said.

"Boy, I'm glad I threw on a little Bad Gal mascara tonight," I said lamely as the flash went off again.

"Yeah," he answered absentmindedly, surely feeling the exhaustion of his long day. "You betcha."

Chapter 13

Driving (Me Insane)

Usually when my husband and I get in the car, I open the passenger door and he opens the driver's side. It's just one of those unspoken, understood agreements. He drives, I sit. And I tell him how to drive sometimes. I have some pretty strong opinions about how he drives.

Now that I think of it, driving a car is a lot like a marriage. Each of you has your role, you know where you sit, you know how he takes corners, how loud he likes the radio, and what stations he prefers. You know that sometimes he doesn't slow down for pedestrians as urgently as you think he should. And you never stop trying to improve those deficits in your loved one.

When you are driving, you have to have a certain amount of trust and faith: trust that you'll get there safely, faith that the other crazy knuckleheads on the road will stay out of your way. When someone else is driving, you have to give up control. You have to believe that the driver will deliver you in one piece, use the necessary reflexes, make the right decisions, and stay on the road. When you look at it that way, driving is a partnership.

Not long ago, I was accompanying my husband to a dentist's appointment. I knew he was tired and in pain, so I insisted on taking the wheel. As I navigated the city streets and stoplights, I began speed-dialing my way around town, periodically glancing at a to-do list half a block long, figuring out calls to make while he was at his appointment.

"Can I speak to Barbara Finder?" I squawked into the phone. "I need to set up my half-year guidance counselor appointment for my son." From the passenger seat, Bob cocked his head at me like a rare bird.

The next call was for my daughter's hearing aid repair, and the one after that was to make an appointment for the car inspection that had silently slipped off our radar screens. That car was now sitting with expired stickers in the driveway and had been for weeks.

"Let me drive, for Pete's sake," he said, annoyed. "Why didn't you tell me you had things to do."

"What are you talking about?" I said. "These are phone calls. And just for the record, I always have things to do. For instance, right now I'm driving you to the oral surgeon."

I was bewildered. This is what women do. It's certainly what I always do. *And,* I thought but did not say, *I'd be doing a lot more if I were home right now, including simultaneously washing dishes and sorting laundry, if you hadn't waited so long to speak up about this tooth pain. Your tooth pain has interrupted my day.* Of course he was allowed to have a toothache. It just wasn't something I'd counted on, and some of these calls needed to get made before it was time to pick the kids up from school.

But all of this makes Bob nervous. It doesn't matter that I'm the queen of multitasking—for him, it's a totally foreign concept. This is because he has been born without the ability to do two things at once. In fact, scientists say they've now discovered that there is a very real physiological explanation for why men can't multitask: they are just not wired that way.

I get proof of this whenever the cell phone rings on those rare occasions when my husband is unloading the dishwasher. As he answers the phone, it's like he drops anchor, wherever he is standing on the kitchen floor. It's a Pavlovian response: phone rings, action stops.

I find it sort of fascinating to watch. Sometimes, just out of curiosity, as he talks, I will guide his body slowly toward the dishwasher again and place his hands on the glasses, the way rehab therapists work with stroke patients. He will make a feeble attempt to refocus, but, for the most part, he will be gone, completely absorbed in whatever he is talking about. This is how he has always been. (His mother claims he was born this way.)

My theory is that this kind of single-mindedness dates back to the dawn of early man. It was critical for survival. Men had one task: they had to go out and club something and drag it back to the campfire for the women to cook. A man's greatest asset was his ability to focus in on that prey with laserlike concentration.

After all, what if man was in hot pursuit of a woolly mammoth but couldn't stop fretting about the upcoming PTA meeting and scheduling the kid's orthodontist appointment? What if, while he was in mortal combat, part of his brain was trying to remember whether he'd defrosted the ground beef for that night's meal or tested his kids on their vocabulary homework before school? That kind of distraction could spell instant death. One moment's hesitation and he'd be shish kebab on the tip of a woolly mammoth's tusk.

Before men get too much credit for this, though, remember that there was another reason why a man could completely focus on defending his cave, killing things, and fighting marauders. When he got back to camp, there was a woman, skinning prey, nursing a baby, and stoking the fire with twigs she had gathered. Prehistoric woman was the supreme multitasker. And in addition to all of that, she had to learn to fend off her man, "the victor," who was most likely hanging around the fire, pawing her, hoping for a little nookie as a reward for his exhausting day of clubbing meat. So prehistoric woman figured out how to multitask the nookie, too.

Modern men do try to keep up. But they're just not born for it. When Bob is in charge of the weekend errands and driving tasks, he begins with the best of intentions. However, as always becomes crystal clear, he lacks a basic sense of time. He imagines that it is possible to accomplish all errands in an hour. It baffles me that he thinks that in sixty minutes he can get gas, hit the grocery store, and run to the boutique with Cathryn, where she will figure out how to coax a cute Juicy Couture top out of him at full price. He approaches each new Saturday (on the days he does do multiple errands) as if it is a blank slate. I try hard not to smile superiorly when my husband tells me he is going to accomplish five things and be back in time to get our twins to soccer all within the next hour.

"That is not physically possible," I'll say to him, "even if you don't obey any traffic laws." I am almost incensed at his certainty, as if this running-errands thing is something he has any real practice at. I can tell he's thinking that a mom can fritter away a whole morning just fetching vittles, going to the dry cleaners, and making a stop for the printer ink cartridges that everyone's computer seems to be out of. But a dad? No way. He is convinced that he can accomplish all of these things in an hour.

And then, somewhere around the second errand, he will return, sheepishly admitting that maybe he was a little "ambitious." After a few mistakes, I have learned that it is advisable to hold my tongue. "I told you so" doesn't have much of an upside in a marriage.

However, what's fair is fair, so, on the driving front, I have to state for the record that I was born without any sense of direction whatsoever. I could get lost in a parking lot, and I have. There is absolutely no homing system in my entire brain, and many of the times when I've been sure that I was absolutely right, I have been so dead wrong that

I've ended up in neighborhoods I was lucky to get out of alive. I will be the first to admit my failings—before my husband beats me to the punch.

In the old days, even when Bob thought he knew exactly where he was going, we would find ourselves sparring with each other. He would thrust the map at me in the passenger seat and I would desperately try to decode it before we missed the next turn because he was incapable of *pulling over and stopping*.

It was hard, in these moments, not to recall the road trips of my childhood. Packed into the back of the Oldsmobile Vista Cruiser with a "moon view" bubble top and simulated wood paneling, our voyages predated seat belts. During vacations to unfamiliar places along the east coast, we were the seventies version of a pimped-out ride, complete with sleeping bags, board games, snacks, and books. We even had a small, portable potty with red and white peppermint stripes, shaped like a giant KFC bucket so that my dad wouldn't have to continually stop for three little girls. I remember mastering turns with burning thigh muscles while sitting on the potty, the contents sloshing dangerously beneath me.

In the front seat, map spread out on her lap, my mother's anxiety and agitation would ratchet up in the face of all those colored lines as my exasperated father tried to navigate and drive simultaneously.

Clearly, my disability was genetic. And under this kind of pressure, I had to let go of my dignity pretty darned fast and admit that my brain didn't work this way on command; I needed to get "oriented." Bob would start shouting out coordinates and highway colors and numbers. It was mildly humiliating, even though I recognized I'd done poorly at any kind of grade school geography, and his tone was one people would use while rubbing a puppy's nose in its tinkle puddle on the carpet. It seemed impossible to him that I could really be so inept. This was not the time to remind him of the dishwasher/cell phone phenomenon.

Naturally, the more frustrated I would get as I searched desperately for the missed intersection or exit on the map, the faster we would barrel forward, missing chances for course corrections. The frustration would build because he *would not stop.*

But the Gods of Driving have shone on the geographically impaired at last. They have given us GPS. Ultimately, it was the invention of that great satellite in the sky, now accessible to mere mortals, that has dramatically improved our marriage.

Everything has changed with the addition of a new woman in our marriage. Just like Princess Di's famous pronouncement, there are three of us in this marriage. Now we have "Bossy Boots," the GPS lady who lives in the black box in our car. Helpful as she is at times, she simply won't shut up. Bossy Boots sounds vaguely, smugly British, and she is a know-it-all.

She breaks directions down into yards and intersections, lefts and rights, and in my husband's eyes, she is omniscient. She can do no wrong. Her slightly superior, sanctimonious tone makes me want to pull her perfect ponytail, bitch-slap her a tiny bit, or yank the strand of white pearls I imagine she wears around her thin chicken neck.

A typical ride with her, at least when I'm the driver, goes something like this:

"After one hundred yards, make a left," she commands.

When I don't, because I trust the written directions that have been dictated to me over the phone, Bob begins to get apoplectic.

"She said to make a left," he whines, upset at my disobedience.

"But the directions I have say to go straight," I say firmly.

"But I trust her more than your directions," he says offhandedly. That's it.

"Fine," I sputter. "Then marry her!" After that, we ride in silence.

When I'm driving alone in my car I like to rebel against Bossy Boots, do little things, take some shortcuts she doesn't know just to irritate her. "Turn around, turn around, make a U-turn," her robotic voice says; she begins to get agitated if I haven't punched in new coordinates. To me, Bossy Boots is a necessary evil. She works my last nerve some days, but looking at the big picture, I understand that she is good for my marriage. At least when Bob is driving.

I've noticed that most people seem to have a female GPS navigator. I have a secret suspicion that certain men enjoy feeling like naughty boys when they are alone in their cars. This satisfies some deep-seated animal need to be yelled at by a powerful woman. And to yell back.

There must be legions of frustrated male drivers screaming back at their female GPS systems, saying the very things they'd love to bark at their wives when they try to tell them how to drive. Berating that electronic voice must be somewhat soothing after a long day at the office. And most important, she can't talk back or withhold sexual favors for bad behavior.

For other men, perhaps she is that nurturing voice they don't always get at home when their spouse has wrapped up a long day of mothering and mind-numbing household chores. This theory was bolstered when a male friend recently confided to me that he loves his GPS. "She keeps me company when I'm alone in the car," he admitted sheepishly.

"Does she have a sexy voice?" I probed, half-joking. He nodded. "And do you picture her?" He nodded again, his cheeks beginning to color.

"So, what is she wearing?" I continued, clearly on to something.

"Lingerie," he answered seriously, hanging his head as if he'd been caught looking at online porn in his den. "Black and lacy."

Ladies, here's my advice: Don't ask and they won't tell. Leave them to their little fantasies when they're alone in the car.

My son recently got his license. As he drove off on his first solo cruise as a free man, I wondered what this new generation of motorists would be like, living their whole driving lives with the constant companion of a disembodied GPS voice. Maybe there would be no more bickering, no more pouting, no more Lucy and Ricky Ricardo moments, no huffy Mexican standoffs over map reading.

This generation would just plug in an address, like pilot and copilot, and go. They can locate bathrooms, hotels, gas stations all from the comfort of their cars. Maybe they would operate in solidarity against the GPS—it would be two against one when the voice screwed up or got confused or demanding. Would future generations even learn how to read a map or would that skill disappear through evolution? (Not that my map skills represent the top of the gene pool.) Would they know about blue highways, choose to look at countries topographically, or pore over coordinates and convert inches into miles to come up with the best route? Would they experience the joy of discovery that I'd had as a kid, studying the crisscross of veins on a state map and searching for towns with giggle-inducing names like Tightsqueeze, Virginia; Bowlegs, Oklahoma; Monkey's Eyebrow, Arizona; Hot Coffee, Missouri; and Glasscock, Texas?

How would they ever envision the whole route, develop a good sense of direction when a disembodied voice was standing by, ready to tell them anything they needed to know? Perhaps GPS would operate the way calculators had, by eliminating the need to keep more complex math skills fresh, or the way texting and IMing are fast replacing phone calls and face-to-face conversation. My Lord, what if the damned thing broke?

But perhaps, in the end, there would be fewer divorces, less domestic violence in my children's generation, I reasoned. And as Mack confidently punched in the address of the away soccer game, threw his duffel bag in the backseat, and zoomed off toward the highway, I took comfort. Maybe he would simply be more highly evolved.

Chapter 14

Pet Hell

Bedtime for me is like running the last few hundred yards of a 10K. The kids are washed, the stories have been read, the blankets are snugly tucked under chins, and my little angels are barely conscious. I'm tiptoeing out the bedroom door, seconds away from a sliver of solitude and maybe a glass of wine, and then I hear it.

"Mom, when can we get a dog?"

Bam! I sprain my ankle just as the finish-line tape breaks across my chest. When all of my defenses are below sea level, my daughter Claire can sense weakness the way a shark smells a paper cut.

From almost the moment she could speak, Claire started asking for a dog. She was simply a girl born to have a dog. She would be happy *being* a dog if fate had doled that one out.

I smile patiently from the doorway. "Mommy has her hands full, Mommy already has four kids and a daddy. . . . Mommy will be the one taking the dog out to pee in a blizzard. . . . Mommy has sooooo much

love in the house already, we just don't need any more love . . . do we?"
I imagine that this scene has been played out in thousands of American homes as regularly as rolling the garbage to the curb. But my excuses were not holding back the nightly refrain. Actually, it seemed to be getting worse.

Before you get your knickers in a twist, let me come clean and tell you that I am just not a pet person. Don't get me wrong: I like dogs, specifically other people's dogs. I like dog paintings, embroidered dog pillows, and I recently bought iron dog doorstops. I just don't want my own real live dog.

I realize this puts me in the minority of Americans. I didn't read *Marley & Me* or mist up at *Old Yeller*. Okay, I was a little jealous of Timmy's relationship with Lassie, but Lassie wasn't your run-of-the-mill dog. And, frankly, I was too young then to realize the kind of damage Lassie's long hair would wreak on a rug or a living room couch.

Here's the thing: I figure I already have pets. The two-legged kind. Taking care of four kids and one husband is a lot of work. And not all of them are properly trained. In fact, the way my family leaves the house—clothes out of hampers, rooms ransacked, shoes strewn all over the mudroom—most folks might assume we'd been given five minutes to evacuate the home after the CDC declared it a hot zone.

And now that my youngest kids are potty-trained and are sleeping in, why should I replace that short-lived bliss with a new family member who needs to be walked at the crack of dawn? Why commit to spending each morning, pre-coffee, scooping up piles of poop and to coming home late after a few glasses of wine in my little black dress and heels to do it all over again?

Honestly, I've seen those parents, the non-dog people like me who have caved under pressure. I've seen them and, frankly, openly pitied them in every neighborhood I've ever lived in. They were the mothers in the housecoats and boots in freezing temperatures with long-handled pooper-scoopers and empty blue plastic *New York Times* sleeves in their hands. Their kids had promised, promised, crossed their hearts and hoped to die that they would take care of the dog if only Mom would relent. But there those moms were, cradling the steaming lump that had been deposited on the neighbor's snowy front lawn at six A.M. And where were the kids? Sound asleep in the comfort of their warm beds. Some battles, those poor moms knew, weren't worth fighting morning after morning.

I'm not allergic to or afraid of dogs. I wasn't chased on the way to school by a Doberman, and I don't sneeze when I go near a dog bed. I'm not immune to swooning over a brand-new puppy with big brown eyes. I just know what it will come down to if we fold a dog into our family: it will be another pile of poop for me to scoop.

It's not that I never gave the pet thing a shot. I had pets growing up. My mother was severely allergic to animal hair and "dander," as she always technically referred to it, so dogs were never an option. Although I wonder now if that whole thing wasn't just a huge ruse invented by a mom who had no intention of caring for one more thing. She got that particular argument out there early, while we were young and impressionable. Why hadn't I thought of that?

So, instead of a dog, I had those creepy bug-eyed goldfish that swam in circles and all died an early death. My sisters and I held elaborate burial ceremonies in the backyard until the day a neighborhood cat dug one up. After that we just flushed them down the toilet, and I often imagined them flowing through the great maze of pipes and ducts under the streets of our town, heading to the giant sewage-treatment plant, where they'd reunite with all their other unfortunate kin—and countless unmentionable toilet-related items.

I also had little green turtles, the kind you could buy at Woolworth's and hold in the palm of your hand. But then people discovered that they carried a disease on their shells, and you had to wash your hands every time you touched them or you might end up convulsing on the wall-to-wall shag carpet with some kind of exotic jungle fever. So they didn't last for very long.

I had a gerbil once, too. I called him Brown Strombus, after a seashell—in case anyone needed proof that I was an odd, bookish kid, trying to memorize the names of all of the world's shells. But then Brown Strombus got loose from his cage and fled under the basement stairs. When I put my head down there to look for him and coax him out, he swiped me with his claws and cut my nose open. I can no longer remember if we ever found Brown Strombus. I may not have cared much at that point. You feel pretty low after your own gerbil attacks you. Even if he was the Rambo of rodents.

After college I tried one final time to be a pet person. Much to my roommate's dismay, and without consulting her, I spontaneously brought home a kitten after a weekend out in the country. I named him Spatz, since he was white with little black feet.

We quickly learned that Spatz had mental issues. He was unstable. These were the days before your vet could prescribe pet Prozac. Perhaps he was an outdoor cat at heart, a free spirit unsuited for a one-bedroom New York apartment. Whatever the cause, he ate my roommate's Walkman headphones twice and then climbed all over the hanging clothes in my closet, managing to snag and shred the shoulders of every suit and shirt I owned. Spatz now lives upstate.

So, naturally, it would be my destiny to have twin girls who wanted a puppy more than anything in the entire universe. Particularly Claire. Oh, Nora was part of the chorus, no doubt, but it's Claire who became president of the "I want a dog" club.

My husband is, like Claire, very much a dog person. His first dog was Wiggles, a faithful and devoted, if somewhat short-legged, mutt. Wiggles was perhaps not the best sports companion for four boys and mostly followed Bob's mom around, hoping for table scraps. But then poor Wiggles was accidentally crushed in the driveway by Bob's father during a particularly brutal and low-visibility Michigan snowstorm. As the car rolled out of the garage, Wiggles tried vainly to scramble up the snowbank and out of the way, but she kept slipping back. Up she would scramble, but her short legs and even shorter dog nails could find no purchase on the icy bank. There were no witnesses, but Wiggles met an untimely death, and the boys were devastated. This only served to teach me that owning pets led to tears and heartache.

Still, no dog looms in Bob's memory and heart the way Shannon does. Shannon was the family's black Lab, and she is always referred to in mythic terms. "The Lab of Champions," she had "boundless energy" and was "the smartest, most gifted dog in the universe." Shannon was a dog fit for Zeus himself.

Shannon would fetch balls for hours, and she never hesitated to jump into lakes or freezing streams to retrieve. She was the sole reason Bob took up lacrosse. He would throw the ball to Shannon, who would bring it back slimed with ropes of dog saliva; then he would use the lacrosse stick to avoid having to pick it up with his hands.

Shannon lived for twelve years and was even around to play with Mack when he was an infant. She was a devoted dog and, in fact, still to this day, Bob finds a Christmas present or two under the tree from Shannon each year. Somehow, in dog heaven, she seems to know just when he might need a new pair of socks or some underwear. That Shannon was always thinking of others.

But for all her age and saintliness, when Shannon was younger she knew how to get into a little mischief. Occasionally she would break free from the house and roam the neighborhood, rummaging through other people's garbage. And when she found food she'd just go ahead and eat it, plastic trash bag and all. As one can imagine, this presented serious problems for Shannon's digestive tract.

Once the plastic bag began working its way out of Shannon's rear end, it would inevitably become stuck. Passing plastic is no easy task, even for a dog's intestines, which can handle all sorts of semitoxic and disgusting substances. Shannon would get a pitiful look on her face and begin to do a dance that involved skooching around on her hindquarters to try to dislodge the bag. At this point, Bob's mom would have to get involved, grabbing the end of the bag with her yellow dish-washing gloves, steadying Shannon's haunches with one soft leather Pappagallo pump, and pulling, while Shannon extruded the bag like some piece of hot metal on an assembly line. As I have stated before, it's things like this that put Frannie firmly into the category of über-mother. I ask you, who else would pull feces-speckled plastic out of a dog's butt?

So, needless to say, I did not want to cave in. I had already bravely soldiered through the "I want a dog" phase with my two older children. They had protested for a while, until I realized they could be bribed with things that didn't drool with bad breath or need to be walked: iPods, high-tech sport shoes, and silver Tiffany heart earrings. In fact, after a while, neither one cared at all about getting a dog. They shared my canine apathy. They even stood strong with me against their younger siblings' puppy mania.

But my twins kept working on me. The worst part was, they seemed immune to bribery. I bought them dozens of little stuffed-animal dogs, Beanie Babies, and then Webkinz they could feed and nurture. They lost interest. Next I found a giant, life-sized stuffed Lab and a German shepherd with glass eyes. They dragged those things around for months, putting blankets on them, sticking their synthetic fur faces into bowls of real water, and bringing them up to their rooms to sleep. But all this did was remind them of how much better a real dog would be.

They drew dogs, cut dogs out of magazines. I'm even ashamed to say that I bought them retractable leashes and instead of using them on the stuffed animals, they played "dog" with each other. This meant one sister would put the leash on the other and take her for a walk around the house. There would be barking and rolling over. They asked for real dog biscuits in the early years of this game, when they loved to go around the house with no clothes on. The few people who happened to drop in during this phase were greatly disturbed. There were some play-date moms who never called to schedule again.

Three Christmases ago I decided to buckle, partially, and get them hamsters. They were small and furry and lovable and they didn't require much attention—no groomers or kennels or astronomical vet bills. Maybe, I hoped, the hamsters would stave off the dog desire. Plus, my babysitter assured me, they could live in a fish tank. This we had.

There was a lot of initial excitement, but after the girls figured out that hamsters could not snuggle, fetch, or sleep with you and instead liked to bite fingertips, my plan started to fail. And once the skin had been broken, the jig was up.

In less than a week, Claire was back at my elbow, asking, "Can we get a dog?" She was as persistent as a Saks Fifth Avenue perfume sprayer.

"Who needs a dog when we have our hamsters?" I offered weakly.

One night a few weeks later, I was out of town and cuddled up with a book in the hotel room, dealing with the parental malaise that sets in when you get to order room service, take a hot bath, and watch an in-room movie with no interruptions. My cell phone broke through the bliss. It was Cathryn.

"We're home from the movies, Mom," she said breathlessly. Her tone made me sit up in bed. "But you are never going to guess what happened."

"What?" I said, dropping the book on my lap.

"The hamsters had babies!" she yelped. "It's gross. They look like pigs in a blanket. With no blanket."

"What?" I said, dumbstruck. "The guy at the pet shop swore those hamsters were two boys."

Silently I cursed the stoned, acne-faced teenaged delinquent with the Mohawk and multiple piercings who had assured me we were buying two male hamsters. The hamsters had been snuggling all right, just not with my girls.

"But, Mom," Cathryn wailed, her voice rising dramatically. "The hamsters ATE some of the babies . . . parts of them. It is so GROSS!" As if on cue I could hear the plaintive cries of my twins in the background. No one had told me that male hamsters in captivity turned on their offspring. *Great,* I thought. What a fuzzy-warm lesson for the kids about the circle of life. After that, the hamsters began a new life at our babysitter's home. Out of sight, out of mind.

And so it continued: the pleas, the babysitting dogs for other people, the visiting dogs, the pet shop field trips, the buying a puppy book. My resistance began to feel like it was bordering on child abuse.

"Don't do it," knowing friends said. "Are you crazy? With your life? You don't need one more thing," they cautioned.

But, I reasoned, I had liked Shannon, trash bags notwithstanding. There was a genuine place for her in my heart. I could envision that kind of attachment and affection. Still, large dogs make me nervous: big, slobbery, hair-shedding things with gobby strings of mouth snot trailing from the corners of their lips. I've always found big dogs to be crotch sniffers, too. Either that or my crotch smells like steak.

So it was clear that if we did decide to get a dog—and I say *if*—it would have to be a little dog. Little dogs have small poops. But they also tend to come with funny names, especially since people are crossbreeding them now the way biogeneticists create broco-cauliflower and seedless watermelon.

Out there in dogland, big dogs are getting it on with little dogs, poodles with dachshunds, Dalmatians with bichons frises. There are a lot of "poo" dogs—which I discovered means part poodle. Poodles always seem to be in the mix. There are Labradoodles, cockapoos, doxipoos, and schnoodles. This makes me think the poodle likes to get around. He is the porn star, the Johnny "Wadd" Holmes of the dog-breeding world.

Without committing to anything, we looked online at terriers, Cavalier King Charles spaniels, Havanese, and finally shih tzus, and for a while, my girls were fixated on that last breed. Personally, I think they just wanted to say the word *SHIT-zu.* It's just too fun. Kind of like giggling at fart noises in the back of the station wagon.

So there we were. Coming up on the twins' eighth birthday. I could feel myself weakening.

And then I did it. I said yes.

"You can get a dog," my birthday card to them said, and it came with two exorbitantly expensive leashes, the price equivalent of a half day of swanky spa treatments. I instantly became the world's best mommy. They looked at me in disbelief. It was like one of those Miss America contests when the finalist takes a full beat to realize the immensity of the judges' decision. She has won. And then she begins to shake and cry, the crown slipping from her perfect mane, her body wracked with sobs. Okay, so it wasn't that dramatic. But it was pretty darned close.

"My life is perfect," Claire announced to me in the car the next day.

"Well, that's great, honey," I said. "I'm happy too." Mentally I was cataloging the ripped furniture, the scratch marks on my newly painted front door, the spilled water dish, and the ash-gray dried poop piles that would soon be dotting my yard like land mines. But I had already said yes and there was no going back. I'd blown up the bridge over the canyon behind me.

Just a few short weeks later, we welcomed Woody into our house. And as these stories so often go, the old grouch, the skeptic, became the convert. An eight-week-old Coton de Tuléar—yes, we went the breeder route—Woody fit the bill. He is a small dog—small poops, no tumbleweeds of hair blowing across the living room, and absolutely no yipping. I felt the ice floes begin to defrost around my heart when I held him the first time. Me, the non-dog person, with a breed whose name I couldn't even pronounce, flipping through canine training books with the intensity I'd used to summon for cramming for college finals.

Now I rise with the rest of the new-puppy moms at five A.M. to take Woody out to pee. I say things that were once unimaginable, like "Mama loves her wittle wittle Woody-poo" and "Go pee pee now, Woody-woo, make Mommy happy!" This was the kind of sickly saccharine talk that used to make my skin crawl when I'd pass dog people.

Recently I got suckered into some expensive accessories, like doggie towels and beribboned collars. I am the Paris Hilton of the over-forty pet set, although I draw the line at dog barrettes and sweaters. I ask people if I can bring my dog with me when I visit, so loath am I to leave him home alone in his crate. I have even brought my dog to a business meeting, sneaking him into the office building, past the lobby guards. I have become one of *them*.

That first week of Woody's arrival, as I tucked Claire in one night, she threw her arms around my neck and squeezed me tight.

"I don't have any more dreams, Mom," she told me. "They have all come true."

I hesitated briefly, wanting to remember the sweetness of the moment and I crawled in next to her.

"You will have more dreams, honey," I answered. *And they will be more expensive,* I thought to myself. But there wasn't anything she could have said that would have made me happier right then.

Claire turned and rolled over under her blanket, toward the wall, as I gave her a final kiss. Me? I headed downstairs to give Woody one last stolen snuggle and take him out to pee . . . knowing I'd be up at dawn's first light to check if he'd pooped in his crate.

Chapter 15

My Dad

have a photograph of myself in kindergarten. I know it's from Thanksgiving, as I am posed in front of the fireplace, dressed as an Indian, wearing an upside-down paper grocery bag, a hole cut through the bottom, out of which pokes my head. The rest of the bag forms the dress, and the hem is cut and fringed. With paint or heavy crayon—the black-and-white photo is slightly fuzzy—I have drawn a sloppy design on the plain brown paper. A lone feather sticks out of the top of my headband, bobbing above my bangs, and my Quaker Oats–can tom-tom and homemade drumstick are held in one hand. The other rests jauntily on my hip, as I gaze at the photographer, my father, with a wide, gleeful smile.

With my pixie-cut blond hair and black patent leather shoes I am a cigar-store version of the Indians who warily greeted the pilgrims and taught them that nifty trick with the corn and the fish. I look proud, expectant, and completely at ease, with the confidence of youth. At that moment, the eldest of three daughters, I have the undivided attention of the most important man in my life.

Over the years, as we pawed through the plastic sheets and crackling spines of my parents' photo albums and participated in the annual summer ritual of the family slide show, this one picture would inevitably pop up. Once sharply black and white, that photo is faded now to multiple gradations of gray. The little blond Indian grew up. And, in the inevitable passage of years, as I moved closer to my own adulthood, and then became a mother myself, I began to recognize that I comprised pieces of my own parents, both unbidden and deliberate.

Over the past decade, as the giant seesaw of life began to tilt, I also understood that ultimately I would begin to parent my parents. It would occur by degrees at first, the way a child gains independence, and then more actively as the end stages of life unwound.

The vibrant image I carried of the father who took that picture, the visions in my mind of a robust man, laughing, pushing the lawn mower, or tunneling snow forts in the backyard, had begun to fade into a sepia photograph of long ago. As with the Indian and her homemade drum, time had marched on and the picture had changed.

At this past Thanksgiving dinner, decades beyond that memorable picture of me, my mother handed my father his weekly plastic dispenser of pills, the one clearly marked with the oversized abbreviation of each day of the week on it. I was the cook now; it was my own home, my hearth, and my parents had driven from Boston to celebrate with my family and that of my sister Nancy.

"I don't understand," my father said quietly, handing the bright plastic pill pack back to my mother.

Did he not know which day to choose? Did he not understand the symbols? His fingers had scuttled around the solid plastic edges of the pillbox, unable to open it, trembling slightly. And now he used one hand to still the other, as if he were clutching a wounded bird to his chest. He was smiling, making an effort to smile. He didn't want to alarm any of us, to ruin the meal with some childlike outburst, but his confusion had temporarily broken through the surface.

His expression was so painful to me that I had to look away. Mixed with disgust at himself, and disoriented, close to tears it seemed, and beseeching. I didn't want to see my dad this way. I didn't want to be a participant in my father's slow, undignified slide into old age.

"Aging is not for sissies," my mother used to mutter like a prayer when she would return home from visiting her own father at the hospice facility, his interior riddled with cancer. I remembered recoiling from the smells of that room, the yellowed and sickly skin and his grasping hands under the sheet, reaching for ice chips. And then later, as my grandmother inched toward dementia, hoarding tissues up her sleeve but still able to play beautiful classical music on the nursing-home piano, my mother would say it again, barely audible, under her breath.

Back then, I was a young woman, a sophomore in college. I knew that on a larger, celestial scale my mother was a saint, but her dutiful trips to the nursing home were of no real consequence to me. This was simply what adults did, I thought, and I dreaded our enforced visits to the home, the airless building and the old people, practically pawing at we three sisters, hungrily fixing their eyes on us as if youth were a remedy they could inhale. We hated that place, hated the fake smiles of the orderlies and the desperation of the inmates. I would put those visits out of my head as soon as I possibly could, rolling down the car window the second the door shut for the ride home. None of this, I wanted to believe, would ever happen to me.

In the early days, and even well into college, my dad was the person who could hang the moon. He was tall and fit. He knew everything, supplied the answers to all questions: how far the sun was from the earth, why maple leaves turned colors in the fall. His lean frame hauled objects around: ladders, boxes, the heavy items. He was a traditional father and husband in the true sense of the word. He took out the garbage, fixed things, knew about tools and cars, but he lived in a house full of women.

In our home, we worshipped my father like acolytes. He was a heroic figure whose work and travel schedule brought him in and out of our lives. He was the good cop to my mom's front-line disciplinarian. Food, drinks, newspapers—we were better than golden retrievers.

When we were young, my sisters and I devised a game where we would hear Dad's car pull into the driveway after work and rush to the back hall, poised to pop out from behind the door frame when he walked inside. Although he must have heard us rustling and our muffled giggles, he feigned surprise over and over again, as if it were a brand-new trick.

Careful not to spill, we brought him his gin on the rocks with an olive and learned to give him space while he reviewed the day's news, feet up on the upholstered footrest. It was part of the ritual and comfort of our family in the 1960s. Life was predictable, and there were prescribed roles in our house.

I remember, as a young girl, watching him shave, and wondering whom I might marry someday and share this kind of intimacy with. As he swiped the blade efficiently around his face, the sharp mint smell of the shaving cream and the English Leather cologne filled the air like an exotic, foreign spice.

The summer I was nine, my father built a small cottage on the hillside above his own parents' house on Lake George. This was his dream, his desire for his family to spend summers in the tight-knit community where his father ran a YMCA camp. Simple though the house was, he had been involved in every detail, driving up north each weekend to watch it take shape and, with the mason, choosing each stone for the fireplace.

The fall of that year, on the side of the house, he built us a tepee, using long sturdy branches from saplings tied at the top with rope. I learned to love plants and developed a green thumb from my father's seasons of tending his beloved hanging baskets and planters of geraniums, lobelia, and impatiens. One summer we had a giant vegetable garden in the side yard. Although I'm sure my mother must have weeded and tended to it, it is my father who appears in the pictures with us, holding plump red tomatoes, thick waxy cucumbers, and bulbous zucchinis. It is my father I remember spading the plot of yard and fencing the area off from rabbits. He always had the exciting, proactive roles in my mind, not the routine and daily caretaking that seemed to be assigned to women.

My father's home office was ordered and tidy. Pungent with the oiled-wood smell of his desk, with its stacks of paperwork and plug-in calculator it seemed a place of men, and had a foreign feeling I yearned to understand. There was a picture on a wall shelf, from his days in the army; he'd been posted in Germany in a tank division. The tank logo had been designed by my father. It was a caricature of a bee clutching a bomb—I suppose because he was in Company B. I'm afraid if I ask him now, he won't remember.

My father had an artist's sensibility; perhaps in a different era, he would have pursued architecture instead of engineering. But I remember my awe as he showed us the fine, delicate silverwork he had done in the army workshop to make a replica of the bee logo. It sat on purple velvet in a wooden box in his office, a relic from his carefree days, when all of the important decisions that would define him still rolled out beyond: career, wife, children, desires fulfilled.

In the picture, his hair is in a crew cut and he looks at the camera with an easy confidence. I remember that look in the photo, so alive and cocky, although I haven't seen it in years. His smile is so broad that you can see that his eyeteeth stick out slightly, the way mine did before I got braces. "Fangs," he had called them. "You got your fang teeth from me." And that quirky similarity, that shared defect in our genes, made me feel even closer to him.

In the army picture he is casually holding a cigarette. It is the only proof we have that my father once smoked—just for a few years, he told us. He quit because my mother couldn't stand the smell of smoke, didn't like to kiss him after he'd been smoking, I imagined, or smell it in his hair.

I often marveled at how the mother I knew, who couldn't tolerate it if someone enjoyed a cigarette across the room at a restaurant, could have stood for any smoking at all. The identities of their younger, childless selves, their shared confidences and hopes for marriage, their life before a family seemed mysterious. The photos of my parents dating show a carefree mother I rarely saw under the burden of three young children, a household, and a tight budget to work within.

I thought about the subtle artifice that she must have used, the bravado she must have summoned to show this handsome, lively man that she was game. Ice-skating, washing the car at Flat Rock Stream with a bucket and soap bubbles—these dates and moments are cataloged in the family photo album. My mother, laughing and thin as a model, played the outdoors gal as my father smiled contentedly, consciously covering his fang teeth.

These images of my father showed him in a different light, someone who had once been adventuresome and curious. For this and other reasons, it was my father I chose to tell that I had tried my first cigarette in ninth grade. When he picked me up from a friend's sleepover, I felt a confessor's need to share how we'd snuck a Marlboro after school in the park by the town library. He would understand, although not condone, I reckoned. Most of all, I believed that he wouldn't judge me. He recognized my need to experience the world, so I knew that my admission would be safe with him.

"I smoked a cigarette with Linda," I said abruptly. We'd been talking about something else entirely when I blurted it out. I was sidled up next to him on the one long front seat of the green Buick Skylark.

When I spoke, his profile stayed straight ahead, eyes on the road, as if he was waiting for me to say more before he'd interject. I'd assumed he wasn't going to admonish me, but his silence made me continue uncomfortably.

"I didn't like it very much," I said quickly, and he glanced over at me.

"I just thought you'd want to know, I figure it's something I'd want to know about my own my kids," I added with an absurd kind of wisdom I couldn't possibly have possessed. "I imagine you and Mom think that I might be doing a lot more, a lot worse stuff . . ."

It was the 1970s, and older kids around the neighborhood were experimenting with drugs, protesting the Vietnam War, and no doubt availing themselves of a little free love. As insulated as our household was, none of this could have escaped my parents' notice.

Finally my dad spoke. "Well, I'm glad you told me," he said to me conspiratorially, patting my knee and squeezing my shoulder with his right hand, his left steering effortlessly. "I think that's the kind of grown-up relationship we have." And he winked at me as I wriggled higher in my seat, feeling just a mite older than my years. I had handled this little window onto adult conversation just right.

To this day I don't know if he ever told my mother. She would have had too much class to bring it up to me. Did it hurt her that I didn't take her into my confidence about boys and transgressions and the normal rites of adolescence? She never showed it, never took it out on me or acted glum or grumpy, excluded or out of favor. As a mother now, I understand the kind of restraint and wisdom that must have taken.

It was my father, people said, who was the "people person." I like to think that I inherited that skill from him. He genuinely liked being around people. Those skills got him promoted from textile engineer to salesman to head of sales and marketing at his manufacturing company.

His honest blue eyes, ready smile, and self-deprecating manner put people on a common ground. My dad could work a room as smoothly as any politician—not in an overly animated, oily way, but earnestly, meeting your eyes, offering a firm handshake, making his presence known. He had a kind of guileless humility, which I studied like a textbook. "Treat the waiter the same as the CEO," my dad had told me once, "and you'll probably find something to like about everybody." I had tried to use his approach as a template for living. Often the waiter was more interesting, in any case, and had seen things in life that rounded out the picture. I had attempted to live by his words, and they had served me well.

As little girls, we would sometimes tag along on a Saturday morning as he walked through the textile plant, calling everyone by name. The giant industrial looms rumbled amid the sweatery wet-wool smell to make felt that would eventually be used to weave the giant belts that wrung out pulp for paper making. The manufacturing floor was warm from the constant hum of the machinery, and people moved with sure steps as they executed the repetitive movements of their jobs on the assembly line. My dad called out to each person, introducing us as his girls. We could feel the pride he took in that, in showing us off, our little blond heads bobbing like ducklings behind him as he walked between the red painted safety lines on the wooden factory floor.

When we're seated around the table at Thanksgiving now, though, I see that the family portrait has changed. It is I who am in control. I am the parent—setting the table, organizing the courses, cooking and waiting on my own mother and father, concerned for their comfort.

Somehow, in what feels like just the passage of several seasons, I have gone from daughter to caregiver, growing into the role with my sisters, tentatively, gradually, making decisions and removing responsibilities as in a game of pick-up sticks. I am reminded of gently arranging the blankets up over my own sleeping children.

Watching my father—the pill fiasco forgotten, his smile more settled now, his panic and confusion somewhat damped down—I feel my own anger rise. What a robber, a cruel thief the loss of the mind is. Dementia, early Alzheimer's—even without a precise official name, we knew what was happening. It was an agonizing slipping of the tethers, a chipping away of dignity as memory became unglued. My once proud father had lost his footing, listening but often not hearing, afraid to interject. As much as I could not, I longed to avert my eyes. If I couldn't see it, I reasoned, it didn't happen.

For years it had been my father's summer ritual to get the mail for his daughters in the same close-knit community where we had grown up as children. Each of us had acquired a cottage, all clustered on the same bay, with a family beach at my parents' place, chock-full of grandchildren in July and August.

My dad would drive up to the one-room post office and collect the bundled envelopes of mail for the families, stopping for a cup of coffee at Sal's Store. Winding his way down the road, he would sometimes stay to chat and refill his cup in our kitchens. Other days he'd be in a hurry to get into his garden or down to the boathouse to putter.

Halfway through August, it was my mother who showed up at my house. When I'd heard the crunch of tires on the gravel, I had listened for my father's sure steps but had instead heard the mudroom screen door slam, a hasty, short noise, more unfamiliar.

Her face was hard, grim almost. It was the expression she'd used when we were little and had done something wrong, the face of admonishment. In one hand she held a bundle of envelopes; the other rested on her hip, as if supporting herself for what she was about to tell me.

"Your dad probably isn't going to do this anymore," she said, waving the envelopes in the air as she pulled up a stool.

"He just got confused at the post office," she added in a softer voice as she saw my face. "I think delivering mail for all of you is too much." She announced the news matter-of-factly, and I tried to appear nonchalant. We knew to give these changes, these course corrections a wide berth. I understood how much effort it took my mother to hide the anxiety and trepidation she must have been feeling inside. It was an unspoken arrangement. We all needed to keep our outward emotions on an even keel, to promote the acceptance of "this is the way it is now." To display more than the rudimentary emotion, to offer pity or sorrow might break the dam for all of us.

When my sister Meg went to the post office later to investigate, she learned that there had been a substitute that day. In this tiny town where everyone knew each other, the regular postmistress sorted the mail for our various houses, separating them with a rubber band so my dad could easily distribute them.

Instead, that day, the substitute had handed my father the whole pile, and he had balked. The thought of sorting it all was overwhelming, too confusing. He had come home frustrated and defeated.

My eyes swarmed with tears when my sister recounted this. How had someone once so vital and in control been reduced, by the trick of a cruel disease, to this?

Like me in my own marriage, my mother had been happy to abdicate responsibility for certain things: the bills, the investments, the college funds, the oil changes and annual tire rotations. It was my dad who'd replaced the winter storm windows with the summer screens. These were all things that in her generation fell on a husband's shoulders.

She had kept house and managed our busy schedules, stayed within the budget, shopped for groceries, and cleaned each week. She'd anticipated a retirement full of travel and the luxury of time. My mother had held to her part of the deal, but now the truculence of age and genetics was robbing her husband of his end of the bargain.

My dad's father had suffered a heart attack at age sixty-five, only months after he had retired. He and my grandmother had bought a ranch house in New Jersey and prepared to settle in to enjoy this next phase of life, no longer at the beck and call of his office.

Chopping wood behind the house, my grandfather had been killed instantly by a massive coronary. This family history, this shadow of mortality, had hung around my father like a cloak. I wouldn't see it until I was much older, but deep inside I sensed that he worried that this might be his destiny too. He was as human as the rest of us, and mortality was not something you could best.

I saw my father's tears when he learned his own father had died. Until then, I had never seen him cry. Although he was far from stoic, he had never let us witness his sorrow. Anger, frustration, impatience, yes, but not sorrow. That was a sign of weakness. Any altercations or emotional scenes between him and my mother occurred behind closed doors.

I suspect that in a way his fears rooted him to the spot. Rather than adopting a carpe diem approach to the world, he was cautious, working for the same company all of his life. When the opportunity arose to run a different manufacturing division overseas, he did not take it. Whether that was his decision ultimately or my mother's veto, I don't know, but I viewed him as somewhat risk averse. Born on the fringes of the Depression, he was a product of his upbringing, of the times, I imagined. You take the sure thing, the bird in the hand.

But I wonder, too, if he felt that by staying between the lines in life, he might in fact eke out a few more years. If he did everything right, perhaps he could cheat death as his father had not, and enjoy a retirement surrounded by his grandchildren at the lake.

Yet for all this caution, it was my father, one of the first people my husband and I told of our plan for Bob to quit law and become a journalist for a minuscule salary, who encouraged us the most. I had followed Bob to China the day after we were married, and his career change was happening just after the birth of our first child.

My father had every right to be skeptical about this new venture and this man who was dragging his little girl around the world to follow his dreams. Nevertheless, he was the first to congratulate us both, to give us his blessing. "This sounds like something you need to do," he said brightly.

"And I know you will be successful," he added. "I'm proud of you both, and if there is anything your mom and I can do . . ." I remember letting out a breath at that response. I hadn't known exactly what to expect. He was fiercely protective of all of us, hoping to ensure, as I imagined every father of daughters did, that their son-in-law was worthy.

"I'm so proud of you," he says to me now, every time I see him, when I arrive and leave. His voice is choked with emotion, with the full understanding of just how quickly life speeds up. He says it now to fill up the air, to interject with something relevant or related to the conversation. I always give the same response, a kind of shrug and a smile.

"We're so proud of all that you do," he says again, as he is coming or going or sometimes just sitting still. His pride is palpable, the emotions all there just under the surface. There is simply less armor to protect him at this stage. Feelings and emotions emerge more quickly, just as his skin is thinning to a tissue-like consistency. He bruises like fruit now, big, splotchy, purple bruises where the blood seems to pool just under the surface of the skin. Sometimes in the summer when he works with his hands at the boathouse, I will find him bleeding; he will have cut himself, unaware.

"Your mother and I are so proud of you, Lee," he says again. And I have no answer. It requires no response. But what will I do when I can't hear those words anymore?

What will I do when my father is gone? How will I mark his life when he passes away? I've begun to collect stories of death, ways that children honored their parents.

This past summer we attended the funeral of a family friend. The mother of two boys, she had been a gracious southern woman who fought her ovarian cancer until the end, facing every day wearing the bright red lipstick that was her signature. Her wish had been for a Dixieland band to play at her funeral, to mark the joy she had felt in her life and not mourn the passing.

Another friend had always loved the many multicolored and patterned ties her father had worn. He was an urban doctor with a reputation as a dapper dresser. When he passed away from a grueling cancer, her mother lovingly cut up every one of his ties and made a quilt for each daughter. When my friend needs comfort or guidance or simply wants to channel her dad, she reaches for the quilt.

An acquaintance told me that when her mother passed away, after a long illness, packing up the things she'd worn was the hardest part of saying good-bye. Her mother had been a clotheshorse, a strong, tall woman with a sense of style who'd loved hats—in all colors and shapes, often worn with beautiful silky scarves.

The daughter brought all of the hats and scarves to the funeral and passed them out to her mother's female friends. Delivering a eulogy, she looked out over the rows of women, each with a red, blue, or purple hat of wool or straw, and she felt her mother's presence in each one of those participants. It was a feeling she couldn't describe, she said. A feeling that allowed her to believe that her mother was there that day, sprinkled throughout the crowd, giving her the strength to hold it all together.

What, I wondered, would life feel like in the absence of my father? Although he was already slowly, inexorably leaving us, the finality of death was too painful and difficult to contemplate.

As dementia progressed and I imagined my father lying in a nursing home bed, the way I'd seen my grandparents, I knew that at least he would be present. I could stroke his head or feel his cheek. I could be in the same room with him, even if he had become someone unrecognizable to me and I to him.

He would still be my father, with the same bones that had held me up for piggyback rides and the hands that had walked with fingers like dinosaur legs across a tabletop and then tickled my belly to cheer me up. Somewhere he would always be in there. What would his end be like? Would we feel a complexity of emotions too interwoven to untangle—sorrow, grief, relief, closure?

After that Thanksgiving meal, once the dishes were washed and put away, my sister Nan showed my folks some of the old family photos she had been systematically scanning into her computer to save for all of us. The old black and whites, including the ones of my grandparents, Dad's parents, seemed to delight him, particularly the snapshots from summers past.

When my sister got to the photos of all of us from the 1960s, lined up in descending height at the fireplace in black velvet dresses and patent leather shoes for the holidays, Dad's eyes crinkled into a smile.

"Remember how Mom dressed us that way every year?" she said, laughing as he nodded.

"Dad, do you remember 29 Roweland Avenue?" my sister said hopefully. He looked hard at Nancy, trying to concentrate with all he had, but was only able to muster a vague smile.

"I don't," he said simply.

It had been their first house, the 1950s American dream, a small center-hall Colonial. They raised all three of us there, and it was by that fireplace that I'd stood as a Thanksgiving Indian, smiling in the bright glare of the old-fashioned disposable flashbulb. I'd lived there for the first sixteen years of my life, before my father had been transferred to Buffalo.

One summer he had stripped all the paint off the wood siding himself. It seemed the ladders stood against the house for months; he would return from work, throw on paint-spattered clothes, and sand off the layers of paint lovingly. "Doing it right" was what he always said. "If you're going to do it at all, you might as well do it right." Nancy pointed to a picture of the house, newly painted, with trim black shutters.

"Where is this?" he said, cocking his head slightly.

"Dad, that's Delmar," Nancy said gently. "That's where we all grew up."

Chapter 16

Chutes and Ladders

After every full-blown crisis comes the moment when the adrenaline retreats and the shoulders sag. The person is out of the critical zone. The patient has been discharged from the hospital. The divorce papers are signed. The father has been buried. The chemo has started. This is the moment when the real work begins. This is the "ever after" part—the new life, post-crisis, that cries out for definition.

There are absolutely no shortcuts through sorrow and pain or to mitigating the day-to-day terror of a crisis. There's no going around it. It's like a long, dark train tunnel in the Alps. All you can do is go straight through it. Buckle your seat belt, pray, do your homework, stretch, keep breathing, turn to literature, gather collective wisdom for solace, brace yourself, talk it through, hold on. Grief, loss, and the twisting roller coaster of emotions that accompany it are all about endurance. Sheer endurance.

In my own crisis, this new period began the moment my husband was out of the acute-care stage. Bob had woken up from the coma, but he barely resembled himself. His brain was missing words and names, and he was having trouble tracking conversations. He couldn't say "Tony Blair," but he could pronounce "Mahmoud Ahmadinejad." Each day brought new accomplishments and new worries. He was still very much a patient and not yet back to being a husband and father.

By nature I'm largely a happy, positive person. But in the wake of Bob's injury, I'd been felled by a pretty large ax. There were days when I thought it would be better just to lie down and sleep for a thousand years. Other days I wanted to sell my kids on eBay to a mom who would be more loving and attentive. There were many mornings when I couldn't wait for bed, when I didn't get outside once, when my thoughts and fears fluttered futilely against the side of my brain like bats trapped in a loft.

But I wouldn't allow myself to give in completely to those feelings. For two long months in the hospital I remained up, dealing with doctors, decisions, my four kids, Bob's whole family. Even after Bob awoke from his coma, I approached his care and my relationship with him like a chirpy Doris Day: determined not to let him falter, guarding against his sadness, constantly pumping him up like a manager encouraging a prizefighter from the corner of the ring. Part of my job was to point out improvements, like a scientist studying tiny molecular changes under a microscope.

In particular, I knew, I had to stay positive for the children. Observant twelve-year-old Cathryn, especially, watched my every move. She examined each facial expression and lurked behind corners when I was talking to other adults on the phone. Earlier, during Bob's coma, she even listened in on the call when the neuropsychologist from the hospital was talking to me candidly about the likelihood that we might need to park Bob in a nursing home. She was suspicious and terrified.

Which meant that it was that much more important for me never to let down my guard. But for all my natural optimism, the pressure to stay positive was just a little too much, and as soon as Bob was safely on the road to recovery, I knew I was bound to crash. Every time I rocketed down, I struggled back up; if I'd been up too long, I knew the bad days were destined to inch back. Up and down, up and down my emotions traveled, as if they were playing a game of Chutes and Ladders.

Still, by the time Bob had begun the daily, rigorous schedule of therapy, I knew I was hitting rock bottom. The bad days far outnumbered the good, and I felt like I was in free fall. I would wake up in the middle of the night with all of my deepest terrors flying at me like birds, dive-bombing me with their beaks, and I was helpless to shoo these anxiety attacks away.

When I did manage to fall back asleep on those nights, the sleep was usually fitful. In the morning I would lie there leaden, sodden, and have to force my feet onto the bedroom floor, while Bob snored gently next to me with part of his skull missing, needing every minute of sleep for his brain to keep healing.

Those early moments of the dawn used to be my coveted hours, a time filled with the rich possibility of the day. Instead, I now felt our life as a family cinched tight as a belt, circumscribed by Bob's injury.

Those mornings, I barely held it together while I got the kids dressed and off to school and then my husband out the door to his daily rehabilitation therapy. Finally, one morning when they had all gone, I just collapsed, fell onto the couch sobbing in the quiet hush of my home. These were gut-wrenching, back-heaving sobs. I was crying out the whole last few months and tasting the fear of the unknowable coming years.

It was clear now that, after surviving everything else, I had finally hit my wall. For so long, I had been in "go" mode, always moving forward, making decisions. Like an Olympic athlete facing the toughest race of her life, I had cleansed my body of alcohol, soda, coffee, anything that might dull my senses or distort my mood. I was careful to keep all of the practical parts of me alert, but I had not allowed myself to grieve, or to feel from my nerve endings. And now here I was, back home and with the luxury of time, since the immediate needs of Bob's physical injuries had been handled. The levee was now crumbling.

That morning of my complete despair, my friend Alicia stopped by. She was deeply worried by the new rag-doll me she found on the couch, and as I talked through my darkest fears, I began a spate of fresh tears. What would our life be like? What if his progress just stopped? What if the man who so loved his job, who had functioned as a kind of quarterback, became instead a useless extremity, something resembling more of a mascot than a team player? And the most horrifying question: What if I didn't love him as much in the end? What if my love for him slowly eroded, little by little, if he remained diminished? "I need some help," I croaked. "I need professional help."

"And you may need medication," she said. "In your place I might need medication too."

"Maybe." I nodded, but my one encounter with Xanax, immediately following Bob's injury, had been a disaster. The pill had made me feel dull, useless, and not myself. I'd never liked that out-of-body experience and I didn't want to consider going through that again. I would have been a dismal groupie at a Grateful Dead concert.

After Alicia left that morning, I resumed crying again. And then the oddest thing happened. I closed my eyes and suddenly, a soft, white light blossomed, a burst of enveloping warmth, indescribable but somehow calming. Mysteriously, a feeling washed over me that hushed me, told me I would be okay, this would all eventually be all right. There were no flowing robes and no golden staffs. It was more like an authoritative voice. It was bigger than me, more than me—that's the only way I can describe it now. And in that moment, the terror subsided as quickly as it had consumed me. Once again, I had gone steeply down a precipice and crept back up.

Still, I knew I could trust the light I saw and felt that day on the couch. The mere existence, the possibility of that kind of calm, gave me hope. I didn't need medication, didn't need to numb my mind in order to survive, I thought. Someday I would move through this. As awful as I felt right then, there would have to be better times. Life simply moves on. People adapt, or so I told myself.

Around that time, another sign came to me. This one shook me deeply but ended up giving me strength: my diamond ring broke. When we had lost a child years ago, Bob had given me a small band of seven diamonds, one for every year of our marriage. It had been my idea to remember the child we'd never known and honor the years of our union. All of a sudden, as I was driving to our friends the Bakers' house, it simply snapped. Fingering the roughness of the cracked metal, I looked down in surprise to see the ring intact, but split across the band. I froze at the implied symbolism of this sudden, spontaneous break.

Panicking, I pulled Susan aside as soon as the twins were playing upstairs. "This ring was for us, for Bob and me," I said. "It's broken—does that mean that Bob is broken? Why this timing? Why now?" I needed to understand how this could possibly not augur an ill outcome.

Susan looked at me coolly. "Don't you see, Lee?" she said without hesitating, in her southern comfort accent. "This is actually a good sign. Yes, Bob is hurt, but your marriage is intact. The ring didn't fall off. It's still a circle, and you didn't even lose a stone. It is a symbol, Lee. Bob is going to need to be fixed, he is broken, but it's all still there inside of him."

I will always love her for that interpretation, her soothsaying. Susan had talked me down from the ledge. But my connection to future happiness was so tenuous, so unknowable, that I needed to spread my faith out to encompass everything—to, in effect, hedge my bets. I needed prayers and chants and symbols and omens and objects to keep myself up, to keep myself going. In point of fact, I needed all of the goodness of the universe on my side to pull us through.

While Bob was as fragile as an egg on a spoon in a children's relay game, I hung on everyone's encouraging words. I was the eager, crippled woman in a religious revival tent, riven with sorrow and praying for a miracle. My friends and family, the therapists and doctors, our minister, all of these people were the shamans of my tribe. Although I knew they did not work magic, I desperately wanted to believe they could.

Take care of yourself, everyone said. Make time for yourself, consider what your body needs. But it was impossible. If they could have seen my life, the overwhelming crush of responsibility mixed with all of the little things, the permission slips and school notices, the tax extension and the haircut for Mack, they would have known better than to utter those words. How does any caregiver really make time for herself in the midst of a cyclone? I just hung tight to my game of Chutes and Ladders and waited for the end of the ride.

The months ticked on, and soon Bob was approaching the date for his surgery to place the acrylic skull over his exposed brain. He had lived with a plastic climbing helmet on his head anytime he was on his feet. It would be a long and involved procedure and not without risk. Essentially, they would have to peel back Bob's scalp and lay it over his face as they fine-tuned the size of the acrylic skull plate so that it would fit as precisely as a puzzle piece, then set it into place and use a special epoxy to bond it to his existing skull bone.

He was understandably frightened and anxious. Unlike the dozens of surgeries he had undergone when he was unconscious, he was well aware of this one and its risks. And the thought of having neurosurgery terrified him.

With all of this pressure and worry building up, and everyone still reminding me to take care of myself, I decided I was finally ready to talk to someone. After choosing a therapist near my home, I went for a few sessions. Each time I found myself crying for a solid hour, asking the woman questions she couldn't possibly answer about Bob's ultimate outcome and what would become of us. It soon became clear that my abstract whining in the psychiatrist's office wasn't getting me anywhere solid. She helped me develop some imagery—I was to picture myself on a raft in the middle of my favorite lake—but the night terrors still stole into my room each evening and capsized my calm water scene.

I liked this therapist, I really did, but I found the whole idea of grief counseling disturbing in that, no matter what I was doing or how I was feeling, if it was nine-thirty on Wednesday I had to drop everything and go prepare to grieve. Even if I'd been having a good day, I had to be ready to leave that room after an hour with tissues pressed to my nose, sniffling or holding back sobs. It felt like mourning on cue, and I grew to resent it.

"You need body armor," Dr. Mary Hibbard announced to me one afternoon. Although she was Bob's neuropsychologist in New York, she had agreed to counsel me too. She knew Bob; she monitored and marked his progress. She had concrete answers about brain injuries and examples of other success stories, though admittedly they were few and far between.

"I need more than armor," I told her glumly. "I need an armed personnel carrier." Her suggestion sounded like a nice little euphemism for popping some mood-altering pills. For months I had resisted the idea of an antidepressant, believing that I could find my own equilibrium. Yet something in what she said struck a chord for me. Here I was in a doctor's office sobbing, terrified—I didn't sound so levelheaded at all. And here was a wise woman I respected giving me a practical solution for how to take care of myself, one that didn't require siphoning resources from anyone who needed me. Finally, at that moment, it seemed like a sound rationale. Maybe it was time to seriously consider medication. I was in emotional pain, as one doctor would explain to me months later. And emotional pain is just as real and uncomfortable as the physical kind.

So I agreed to try an antidepressant, since if nothing else it would allow me more peace at night, more sleep, relief from the now-familiar anxiety attacks that seemed to find me as regularly as a Swiss watch.

As it turned out, the Paxil was actually a help. It didn't make me feel like a rodeo clown, or like skipping across four lanes of traffic in a convertible. I didn't have to suppress the desire to sing "The Battle Hymn of the Republic" at the top of my lungs in the shower.

It just made me feel, at last, like me. It resuscitated the old Lee. It created a trampoline under my free fall, a barrier that allowed me to stop myself when I became anxious so that I did not go any lower. It was all very subtle, but over time I began to notice that the fear was more muted and my ability to feel some joy was restored. The anxiety had been driven back down into a containable place where I could talk and reason with myself, using my inner voice. In short, the medication had allowed me to recognize the emerging outlines of the old me.

That prescription eased me through Bob's operation—which was successful—and beyond. And as Bob healed and returned more and more to himself, so did I, although I didn't spend time thinking about the medication.

"Are you still taking those pills?" Bob would ask me periodically, months after that last big surgery, when he was back at work and life seemed finally to be moving in a fairly straight line, with only occasional kinks of uncertainty on my part.

"Yup," I'd answer.

"Why?" he'd respond quizzically. "Aren't we all doing well?" And we were. But if Bob had any little setback—a tired day, a confused moment—if there was any tiny wrinkle that only the expert eye of a wife would see (and I saw everything), it might throw me.

I wanted to take the antidepressants a little longer, I told him. I'd know when it was time to stop, I said. But the truth was, I still wasn't sure. What if now I needed the medication in order to be "my old self"?

I didn't like the idea of taking these pills indefinitely. Not only did they make me sleep a lot more, but I wanted to see what I would be like now that life had calmed down. I wanted to kick out the crutch and see what Lee looked like in the aftermath of a crisis. It would be Lee raw, Lee without the lift.

Could I still have a bad day and then simply recover? Would I be able to go to bed and tell myself that tomorrow would be an improvement—and then really make it better? I wanted to know.

In the past, I had always had the power to talk myself out of a funk, the way I would buck up other people. I reasoned with myself through bad times and focused on the fact that often good things really were just around the corner, like the moment of peace and light on the couch that one morning, or the hopeful interpretation of the broken ring. I had once had a fairly dependable ability to almost will myself happier by focusing on the small acts that lifted my spirits: an outing to the movies with a friend, a brisk walk down by the nature sanctuary in our town, spoonfuls of raw cookie dough. Would I still be able to do that in the aftermath of a crisis, would I still be able to glimpse a little light at the end of every tunnel? Or had the process deformed and mutated me? How could I tell?

And so one day I simply stopped. I didn't say anything to anybody, but I just stopped taking the pills. I didn't flush them down the toilet or do anything dramatic. I just stopped. In hindsight, I probably should have consulted my doctor first, but I felt certain I knew best what my body and mind needed.

So far, so good, I decided after a while.

Of course I had days here and there where I was down, but they were usually followed by days where I was relatively happy again. I found joy in a cobalt-blue sky, in going for a swim or a walk with a girlfriend. In short, my motor still worked. I still controlled the gearshift, and I still knew how to pull myself out of a tailspin. This was good. This was better than good.

And when a lowish day came by, or something seemed difficult, I talked to myself. I felt for the trampoline floor with my toes, and it was still there. It was not artificial, it had not been medication induced. I had wanted to know that not only could we survive a crisis but that my former set point for happiness could rebound too. And for the most part, it had.

In my life, what the big miracle of Bob's recovery did more than anything was to widen the aperture inside of me to witness the presence of small everyday blessings. The big moments are easy to spot. But the real challenge, the art form, is to find gratitude in much simpler things. We need to be open to feeling the power of a life made up of many little shards of white-light experiences. These moments of grace, as I think of them, are as real and as powerful as the headliners. They help us to throttle up, to rescue ourselves from a nosedive, as surely as those little white pills did for a while for me.

I see these little blessings in the gift of a friend's healthy newborn baby, a clean mammogram, or the really, truly satisfying snatches of conversation I have with my father now, when he is having a good day and can clearly remember the parts of his life. People talk a lot about living in the moment, but to do that, to really achieve that, is to be able to fully participate in all the unarticulated goodness that makes up our lives. And of course, that kind of focus isn't possible every single day. But I try now to give it all my attention when I tiptoe into my children's bedrooms in the morning and stroke their hair as I wake them for school. I count my blessings for having sisters and girlfriends with whom I can unburden and be as comfortable with as a second skin. It is one of life's small gifts to be able to ease someone's pain, to hold their fears for an hour or a day. It is truly miraculous to sit and watch the sun rise and set, or to study the perfection of a colorful spring blossom.

In the second summer after Bob's injury, I could finally say our lives felt secure. It had been eighteen months since our world, like Dorothy's farmhouse, had been rocked off its foundations and gently set down somewhere else. We were not in Kansas anymore. But we were in firmer territory in some ways. We knew the fragility of life firsthand—we lived more in the present; I believe we all did. I was aware of the passage of days and weeks, aware of how finite the time was that I got to be a mom and enjoy my kids on this earth before they became full-sized human beings with independent lives.

None of us would ever choose to rupture the veil of innocence that shelters our children. As a parent I would have liked to spare them from the worst of it, but that's ultimately not realistic. You cannot protect them all of the way. That's not how life works. And that's okay. But in the grateful aftermath of our family's collective sorrow, I tell myself that my kids have learned more from the difficulties and hardships they have witnessed and endured than they ever would have otherwise.

The routes my children constructed to navigate around the fear and loss surrounding their father's injury have forged their capacity to truly engage in their own lives, to be empathetic and to genuinely care for others. I have no doubt that they can already handle situations far beyond what many of their peers can. They have built up the same capacity that now sustains me, the ability to roll down with the chutes and up with the ladders, to reorient themselves and search for hope in even the most terrifying situations.

This fall I was pulling out of my driveway, distracted by the twins, who were not buckling their seat belts fast enough. Nosing into the driveway with spectacularly bad timing was our letter carrier in her boxy white truck. Looking left when I should have been looking right, I suddenly slammed into the truck's side with our brand-spanking-new SUV.

After I made sure the girls were all right I hopped out, mad at myself. The mailwoman was already out of the car, shaking with fear and worried, I'm sure, that Suburban Soccer Mom would start screaming at her. A small wiry woman, she was jumping from foot to foot and swearing as she pulled a pack of cigarettes out of her breast pocket and lit one.

"It's my fault," I said, worried by how distraught she looked. She was already calling her supervisor as we circled around her vehicle. Her old battle-ax of a truck seemed to have suffered only one fresh scrape on the bumper, but my SUV was completely bashed in on the right back side. One of my girls picked up the shattered red taillight housing and handed it to me.

"Damn," the mailwoman said under her breath, shaking her head and taking a deep drag of the cigarette. "My supervisor says he's gonna have to come out."

"Don't worry," I said, calmly. "I'm not upset. Everybody is safe. It's just a car." She didn't look completely convinced. "You can't ruffle me anymore," I said, and I flashed her a smile and reached for humor to calm and reassure her. "My husband was blown up by a bomb. Now, that's something to get upset about."

"What?" she responded, with a physical jolt. "My God . . . is . . . is he dead?"

"No, no," I assured her, "he's fine now. But it makes things like busted cars not that important in the big picture."

"Look at this," the mailwoman said abruptly, lifting her shirt to show me a road map of scars crossing her abdomen and chest.

"Wow." I whistled softly. "What happened?"

"When I was five I fell out of a window and survived. And later I got breast cancer." She gave me a winsome smile, one gold tooth glinting toward the back, and then she took another tug at her cigarette.

"Man!" I said, looking her right in the eyes. "Ain't life a bitch!" And then, right there on the driveway with the broken red plastic taillight, we both just started to laugh.

Chapter 17

What I Know Now

When bad things happen, we all dream of rewinding the tape. Every one of us would go back to the minute before the car skidded off the road, would make the appointment for the colonoscopy a year earlier, would stop ourselves from turning our backs for a second as our child was swimming or when the ladder holding Dad started to wobble.

But we can't, and so we do the only thing we can: we take those bad things and turn them into situations we can learn from. It's human nature to try to pan for gold, to find a positive slant in something so negative, because anything less would feel like defeat. Euphemistically, these tragedies are called "life experiences," but for better or worse, they are some of our most powerful moments.

Thankfully, my own family has come out the other side of our own crisis. First, we survived; then we slowly learned to thrive again. And in the process I have been taught some important lessons about being a caregiver, mother, wife, healer, friend, motivator, and the grateful recipient of oodles of love, goodwill, community support, and prayers.

I am frequently approached by people who have been through very difficult experiences with their loved ones, and after sharing their stories, they are quick to minimize what they have endured in relation to my journey. "But my mother's cancer was nothing like what you went through," they offer. And I disagree. I say that all of this collective suffering exists on the same frequency of human emotion. Grief is not a competition. Sorrow is sorrow and fear is fear and loss is loss and we humans are all traveling on the same bandwidth in life.

In the past year, since the book I wrote with my husband, *In an Instant,* was released, I have traveled around the country and met many people and families who have suffered or are suffering. They have journeyed along what I call the grittier pavement of life.

When I relate what I have learned through tragedy and recovery, I see a lot of heads nod. People want to talk about what works for them and what those who have not walked in their shoes should know.

I have often been asked to share these lessons. Therefore, drawing from my own experiences and what others have told me, I have created a list of things to consider if someone you know or love is facing a life-changing trauma. The following tips, while not necessarily novel, seem to have a universal appeal—perhaps because the big moments, the teaching moments in life, are often a series of unplanned, sometimes catastrophic events with no rational explanation. Because, yes, bad things *do* happen to good people.

1. DON'T HANG BACK—MAKE CONTACT

Though I would venture to say that just about everyone knows someone who has had to face a personal disaster, most people who haven't experienced a tragedy or serious illness at close range have no concrete idea of how best to approach the person who is suffering. They don't know exactly what to say or what to do. Everyone wants to get it just right, but it's frequently hard to gauge what is appropriate.

Coupled with that uncertainty are also very basic, human reactions when someone is sick or injured. Another's accident or illness often seems to threaten our own lives, reminding us of all the frightening possibilities that could befall our family or loved ones. Sometimes these emotions can be paralyzing. But it is crucial not to hang back: the bravest and most wonderful thing you can do is to be there for someone else, even if this takes you completely out of your comfort zone.

When something goes wrong in a friend's life, it is essential to acknowledge what is happening. Call people or reach out when you learn they are ill or going through a difficult time. Don't give up on them if they try at first to push you away, but take your cue from them. If your own emotions won't allow you to engage the person without making them uncomfortable, step back and write a heartfelt note instead. In either case, *do* come back—they will need you later on. Make sure they know you love them and care about them. We all need comfort and companionship. We just may need it at different times and in different doses during the journey.

When Bob was injured, I was surprised by some of the people who stepped into the void in amazing ways to help. In many cases they weren't necessarily the people I had expected. People react to misfortune and mishap in very different ways.

For the people in the vortex of the crisis: it's important to keep in mind that just because some folks don't raise their hands to help doesn't mean they don't care. An inability to cope with what you are going through could simply mean that friends and acquaintances are nervous or anxious about how best to approach you and tackle the situation.

2. HELP THEM FEEL "NORMAL"

When I was living in a hotel room in Bethesda, with Bob in his coma, one of the many fabulous gifts of help came from my friend Kitty, who lived in D.C. We were trying to convert family videos to DVD format to play in Bob's room so that he could hear his children's voices, but we were having trouble. Kitty just showed up, took the tapes, and didn't ask pointed questions or demand information about Bob's condition. She never expected to see Bob in the ICU or to get any inside scoop. She told me about her kids and her husband. She entertained me with stories about her workplace. She just came and helped. Two days later the tapes arrived at the hotel desk, all transferred onto DVDs so we could play them for Bob and help his brain knit itself back together.

My friend Colleen sent me a certificate for a massage, which I ultimately used even though I worried about Bob the whole time. Rebecca came to my hotel suite and quietly filled the fridge with healthful food, arranged flowers near the bed, and organized and prioritized all the mail that had been forwarded. She never asked me one prying question about Bob's condition or prognosis. Instead, she waited until I was ready to talk.

These simple, calming acts and my friends' way of treating me as "normal" were exactly the tonic I needed. In the midst of the tornado raging around my family, I loved it when people talked to me about their aging parents or the fact that their child needed glasses. My world was so unimaginable, I had lost the language of reciprocity. Sometimes when a person's life has changed so much, they want to hear what normal sounds like; they want you to treat them as if their world is just like it used to be.

3. RECOGNIZE THE POWER OF HUMAN TOUCH

When you are visiting the person going through a difficult time, treat him or her like a human being—not a patient. Especially with children, get down on their level and look them right in the eyes.

Don't be afraid to make physical contact. Most illnesses and injuries are not contagious. Touches and hugs are one of the most healing things one person can do for another. Everybody wants to feel like a human being. A loss, illness, or injury gives people a sense of being exiled from the herd, so do whatever you can to make that person comfortable—overlook the tubes and machines they may be hooked up to and just focus on that loved one or friend as an individual.

I remember when Bob and I visited Jose, a young marine with a severe brain injury, in Bethesda Naval Hospital. Since Jose's arms and wrists were still raw with wounds and crisscrossed with tubes, I chose to focus on his feet. I rubbed them as I talked to him, wanting just to give him that basic physical human contact. Jose's mother and sister said that they could see him relax instantly, because someone was treating him like a person and not a patient. Simple acts can go a long way toward restoring dignity to a human being.

4. ESTABLISH A HEALTHY INFORMATION EXCHANGE

This means three things: not demanding information from a patient or caregiver; sharing information that may help a patient or caregiver; and knowing what to keep to yourself.

In moments of crisis, everyone wants information, and many people deserve to get it from the source, since lines of communication can be confusing and not knowing can be terrifying. Luckily, the Internet has made it much, much easier to disseminate information and update family and friends. There are incredibly helpful Web sites devoted to caring for someone, such as CarePages and CaringBridge, which act as a lifeline for friends and loved ones during times of crisis. A person can post messages about their own condition or their loved one's progress on a Web page for others to read. These sites also offer a place where people can write messages of encouragement to a patient, so that he or she can check in when it is convenient. This ensures that the individuals in the crisis don't have to spend precious energy reaching out to everyone, returning phone calls, or even sending mass e-mails.

When you're visiting someone going through a difficult time, don't ask questions that make them recount the whole ordeal, the facts and statistics, or the road ahead. They may not want to talk about the issue at all. Just take their lead when it comes to conversation. Resist the urge to share your own stories about similar illnesses or diseases and other people you know. Many people think that comparisons are comforting or hopeful, but these stories can actually be terrifying or even insulting. More general encouraging comments or expressions of support—such as "I know how hard this is because I watched my mother struggle with cancer"—may be a better way to let the person know that you understand some of what they are going through.

Also, this is not the best time to try to rekindle a two-way friendship that has been a "Christmas card" relationship for years. If you want to let a person know you are there for them, a newsy written note or e-mail with no requirement for a reply is a wonderful gift. It can be digested when the time is right. I loved reading through cards and notes before bed, since it made me feel connected to and comforted by the people who were caring about, and praying for, me and my family.

Some of the biggest gifts were the "Bob stories" people shared with me in their notes and letters. I read about humorous or kind moments people remembered, some I had never before heard about. As with those who have lost a loved one, I cherished these letters over those with general expressions of sympathy because they brought me closer to Bob at a time when he wasn't present.

Ultimately, the best thing you can do is to simply listen to the person you wish to comfort. Be sure to let them know you are there whenever they need to talk, anytime. You don't always have to have a solution or good advice; sometimes people just need to unburden themselves, or simply say things out loud.

5. AVOID OVERMOTHERING

Certain physiological things happen as a result of stress or grief. The normal circuits in the body are altered; adrenaline floods the physical plant, and the endocrine, circulatory, and digestive systems may go through drastic physical changes. The caregiver, as well as the patient, is damaged, in crisis, and sometimes things inside their brains don't work the way they normally would.

Do not repeatedly tell the caregiver to eat or sleep. They cannot. They are operating on adrenaline, especially in the early stages. Food is only fuel, and sleep is hard to come by. And don't try too hard to pry the caregiver away from the patient's bedside for a bite or a walk around the block. They may not ever want to leave their loved one's side, and that's just fine. But also remember that if they say they don't need help with anything, they *do*. Don't be afraid to take charge in nonthreatening ways to ease their daily burdens.

While I was camped out during Bob's stay in the ICU, my friend Lauren knew that I liked decaf lattes, sushi, brownies, and the special corn and crab soup from the hotel room service. In the early days of our own crisis, I would return from the hospital, shattered and in shock, and find these items waiting for me. She didn't nag me to eat or urge me to care for myself; she just took care of me quietly, because she knew I wasn't thinking about food.

Often someone will be designated the point person for the family in crisis. They may be in charge of scheduling meals to be brought in or helping with rides for kids. That person will most likely have a good handle on what needs to be done and what the particulars are. Work through that person and respect that channel of communication, especially initially, no matter how close you are to the individual going through the trauma. That point person is there as an important buffer, to spare the rest of the family or the patient from the unnecessary details.

There are wonderful Web sites like carecalendar.com, foodtidings .com, and livestrong.lotsahelpinghands.com that allow people to sign up to deliver meals or to help with care for others. For the caregiver, this makes the job of assembling a network easier; volunteers can log on at home and participate as needed. And for caregivers and family members of the ill or injured, there are now informational Web sites that can help empower them with useful tools that can be downloaded. Partnersagainstpain.com, for example, provides printable templates for pain diaries and medication schedules to help caregivers stay organized. If you are not a family member or close personal friend, helping from a respectful distance, at least initially, is often the best course of action.

6. BE SENSITIVE TO WHAT THEY NEED TO HEAR

Don't be afraid to acknowledge the person's pain. It's okay to say "This stinks, but I'm here every step of the way." The most helpful comments you can make involve letting the patient or friend know they're being heard.

This is a delicate balance because you don't want to minimize things with trite greeting-card philosophy, but nor do you want to underscore the dire nature of the person's situation. This is where you need to use your sixth sense and assess where that person is, emotionally, at any given moment. It may seesaw from hour to hour. Take your lead from them about what you think they need to hear. It's always comforting to be told, "Let's talk about you for a moment—I'm here to listen if you feel like unburdening."

One of my most precious e-mails at the time came from our friend Jim Wooten, a colleague of Bob's at ABC News and a veteran reporter and writer. It arrived at a time when I was tired of hearing about how incredibly strong I was but, rather, just needed to hear that I could simply do this. That it was all possible. Jim wrote,

> My only counsel to you is this: make sure to take as meticulously good care of every aspect of your beautiful self—physically, emotionally, and psychologically as you do of Bob and the children. I can't stress too much how important that is for both the short and long term, and for everyone involved. You must already understand that you are the most critical component in this difficult equation; and without you as a vibrantly healthy person, it gets even more difficult . . . and, dare I say it, maybe impossible.
>
> I told you in the hospital that my mother-in-law had a motto about her own life, with all its ups and downs: *You play the cards you're dealt.* I realize in retrospect that it was a fairly silly and perhaps a slightly cruel thing to say to you, especially given the awful cards you've been dealt in the last three months. It's possible that the best approach really is to never stop trying to get your hands on the deck and start dealing them yourself. In other words, to begin determining, to the degree possible, your own destiny and direction. . . . It seems to me that the more you're in control, the less disappointed you'll be in what goes on.

I printed that e-mail out, and it still makes me cry when I read it and sense the kindness, empathy, and honesty embedded in the message, the stark and simple concern for me above all else at that moment. I taped the e-mail to the window over my computer at home and vowed I would never stop trying to get my hands on the deck. And somewhere, in that grueling process, I would try to set an example for my children in the midst of this frightening tailspin.

7. THINK PRACTICALLY ABOUT WHAT PEOPLE REALLY NEED

Food, in any time of crisis, is one of the most useful gifts. People have to eat if they want to keep going. This is also true in a hospital setting, since it can be used to thank the nursing staff and win friends among the medical professionals. A batch of brownies works wonders at improving the speed with which a call to the nursing staff is answered. The "Brownie Lady" in room 205 also has a much better chance of being on the radar at the nurses' station in those wee hours of the morning when a loved one needs pain medication.

However, for those of you putting together food chains for friends, remember that you don't necessarily need to schedule dinner every single day. Most folks are very generous, and the leftovers begin to pile up. I ended up feeling guilty as I gave away—and sometimes even had to throw away—food that people had so lovingly prepared.

It also frustrated and disturbed me when my kids would lift the foil on the pan and groan, "Not lasagna again!" It's hard to write this and not sound ungrateful, but if you are going to go to the effort of making someone dinner, try to find out from the point person what others have brought over that week.

Stuffed animals, large objects, and flowers in the hospital are cheery, but they often translate into things that just need to be moved from room to room or take up space in cramped quarters. Consider practical gifts instead, like pajamas, a luxury soap, a new toothbrush, or slippers. A set of thank-you notes is one of the most useful and helpful gifts you can give the patient.

Also, don't tell the patient or caregiver to call you if they need anything. That puts the burden of asking for help on them. Instead, suggest something specific you can do to help out: a ride for the kids or a sleepover, a dinner brought to the house (without dishes that need to be returned), cutting the lawn, or walking the dog. Make decisions for them on the details as much as possible. This includes whether or not they'd like chicken or fish. Just do it!

8. CHOOSE YOUR WORDS AND ACTIONS WISELY

Resist the urge to repeatedly tell the person, "You are so strong." They don't always feel strong, and they don't want to have to act strong in front of you or hold back tears so as not to disappoint your expectations or impressions of them.

And don't expect the patient or caregiver to immediately return your phone call or e-mail. All of their energy right now is focused on themselves (if they are the patient) or their loved one and their other immediate family members. They are being interrupted about every fifteen minutes by medical staff of all sorts, they are talking to doctors, undergoing procedures, perhaps worrying about their children or elderly parents, tending to the immediately critical tasks at home, and, overall, being torn in many directions.

With each concerned phone call I got from a friend who told me that they just needed to hear my voice, I felt more inadequate. "Call me," well-meaning friends would plead into my answering machine. "I have to know what is happening." All that did was pile one more ounce of guilt and failure on my shoulders and add to my to-do list another thing that I knew I wouldn't be able to accomplish—definitely not that day, or maybe ever. If you feel the need to reach out in the midst of the crisis, just leave a message that starts with "You don't need to call me back, I just wanted you to know I am thinking of you."

Also, don't approach the family or patient with tears in your eyes or what I call the "sympathy face" (the hangdog look that says "You poor thing, bless your little heart"). This makes the person feel as if they have to use precious energy to buck *you* up. If you can't keep your tears or overpowering empathy to yourself, come back when you can or write a note.

After we'd gotten Bob home from the hospital, I made my first foray out of the house to the local YMCA for a swim. I was afraid to face the well-meaning sympathy and curiosity in people's eyes, and I didn't want everyone to ask me how Bob was, because I didn't have a definitive answer beyond "He is healing."

I was fragile and timid. I hunched my shoulders over so far I was basically hugging myself as I walked into the locker room. All of a sudden, sailing into my personal space with a giant blond mane and more energy than a Dallas Cowboys cheerleader, was a woman who, to this day, I do not know.

"HOW IS YOUR HUUUUUSBAND?" she screamed, eyes bulging with concern. All heads swiveled toward me. I felt ambushed. My heart started beating wildly, and I simply grunted, doe-eyed, and fled out the locker room door. I understood that the woman thought she was being helpful or thoughtful, but I needed to be approached gently and wanted desperately to be treated like a "normal" person, the person I used to be.

9. UNDERSTAND WHERE FAITH BELONGS

In our own journey, faith, family, and friends played a pivotal role in helping all of us to heal. But faith, especially, means different things to different people. And in the midst of a crisis, people often experience a wide range of emotions.

In the absence of just the right thing to say, there are pat phrases others fall back on that can sound downright irritating, especially if a test result or diagnosis hasn't gone the right way or an individual's emotional strength is ebbing. Try not to say, "God doesn't give you more than you can handle," "Things happen for a reason," "What doesn't kill you makes you stronger," "There but for the grace of God go all of us," "He or she is in a better place now," or "There's a special place in heaven for you." In fact, scrub these phrases entirely from your vocabulary. The person or caregiver doesn't want to feel like Job, wonder why God chose them for this particular rough assignment, or envision a handicapped-parking sign in the hereafter. Be sure not to say things that make a person feel isolated from the greater community, or different from everyone else. Also, keep in mind that while spiritual comfort can be helpful to some, it may come off as irritating or overly personal for others. Make sure you know where people stand on the issue of faith before raising it.

When my friend Gretchen asked me to write some tips for her Web page, to help people cope with approaching her after her son's cancer diagnosis, I gave her this list. She read it, then asked me to take out number 9. She thought it was a bit insensitive to circumscribe people's good wishes and best intentions. "Just wait," I said.

Two weeks into her hospital odyssey, she called and timidly asked me to put this tip back in the blog. We had a good chuckle and she vented for a while. Clearly, she was fed up with trying to catalog the reasons why God would ever give a small child a life-threatening disease.

10. BE THERE FOR THE LONG HAUL

In the first days and weeks of a crisis, people come out of the woodwork, flooding you with offers to help, with food and flowers and kind encouragement. This is wonderful, but it can also be overwhelming. The real work begins when all the neighbors have gone back to their own lives, and the patient and family still need occasional support.

Flowers, for instance, are *very* cheerful in a hospital room. But their effect can be even greater if you wait a few weeks, or even a month or two, and send them to the home. At that time the patient and the family can focus more fully on the beauty of the gift. It is also often a time when they feel as if many people have retreated; there is no one gathered in the kitchen anymore or answering the phone. This simple gesture will make a big difference after the crush of the crisis and will let them know you are still thinking of them. (Those of you reading this who for years have sent flowers to homes and hospital rooms in the immediate wake of an accident or injury, take heart—there are no truly wrong acts of kindness.)

In the midst of our family's crisis, a wise friend told me to subscribe to the "chit system." Immediately after a diagnosis or incident, everyone will rush in to ask what he or she can do. "Tell them they have one chit," my friend Tom said. "And that you will use it. It may be the next day or even two months from now, but at some point in time you will call in that chit."

It could be as simple as bringing over a pizza or driving a kid somewhere—or as complicated as dropping everything and being by someone's side, no matter what. Once, I asked a friend's husband to come over and check our water heater. That used up his chit.

What was great about this concept was that when all the cars had left the driveway and most people had gotten back to their regular lives, I didn't end up feeling abandoned or clingy. And, hopefully, no one person felt overburdened in the long run.

Plus, it made friends feel that they were needed and gave them a task, even if it was two months from the time they'd offered.

And it made me feel like I wasn't a beggar, constantly asking the community for various favors. But all of the people who wanted to help eventually had their chance. To be needed in that way is perhaps the greatest honor of being a true friend.

Three years after Bob's injury, we have all come out the other side, each member of my family. We are all unexpected experts at surviving. We're no different than so many American families: we've acquired scars, opened our eyes, we've grown and stretched, we've ached and rejoiced. We've felt loss keenly, and we've counted our many blessings. None of us will ever underestimate the power of love, family, faith, friendship, and the resilience of the human spirit. Through it all, we've been grateful to have kept our sense of humor and our general optimism intact. We may be messy at the edges some days, but we are a family firmly united at our core. In the end, we are proud to be wonderfully, perfectly imperfect.

Acknowledgments

I've been writing magazine articles for many years about family life and motherhood as seen through my prism. There's a fine line between illuminating a collective experience and betraying personal information. And so I thank my family and friends for allowing themselves to appear in these pages, hopefully with their dignity intact.

This book grew out of a lifetime of little moments, which, after all, is precisely what makes up a life. And these essays are for everyone, myself included, who once believed that if we colored inside the lines, played fairly, followed the Ten Commandments and the Golden Rule, studied hard and worked even harder, loved generously and laughed from the diaphragm, we could script our lives. In the end, no matter what path we all take to get there, life remains truly impossible to predict and wonderfully, perfectly imperfect.

Unconditional love and kudos to my kids, who allowed me to profile their wisdom and foibles in order to help mothers everywhere recognize that we are not, in fact, alone out there. And, my children, for those moments that may embarrass you in retrospect, remember: I gave you multiple chances to read the manuscript!

My love and appreciation go to my sisters, Megan and Nancy, whom I cherish with the weight of an anchor's chain. And to my parents, Dave and Terry, who were the first people to love me completely. Mom, you taught me the definition of devotion, and Dad, you endowed me with a keen interest in people and all of their multisplendored differences.

To Fran and Bob Woodruff, the best in-laws a gal could ask for: your love for and dedication to your four boys is nothing short of inspiring. Mom, you taught me that "it only takes a minute," whatever the task may be—driving a child to college or doing five loads of laundry. Dad Woody, I love you for leading with your heart. To Dave, Mike, and Jim, for being the brothers I never had. And to Lee Ann and Amanda for their collective sister-in-law wisdom. To my Colgate friends, who will always be my root system and my scaffolding. To Rita, Kelly, and Liz as well as Laura, Kerri, and Liza, for girls' weekends that put the laughter back in my lungs and the mojo back in my writing.

Thanks to Bob Barnett for making his magic. And undying gratitude to the folks at Random House who were all my sounding board and sometimes my muse. My editor, Susan Mercandetti, helped me cut and shape and told it to me straight when something simply didn't work. And to Abby Plesser, who offered sage and hip advice and assured me that this was a book for "young people" too. Thanks to Gina Centrello for her vision and support and Millicent Bennett for her perspective, Dennis Ambrose for his diligence and Sally Marvin and Kristina Miller, who always had my back on the road.

Kisses and gratitude to my friend Ali Wentworth for helping me turn up the heat.

All my love, of course, goes to my Bob, for being there in all the big ways and so many of the small ones and for forcing me to look at the glass as half full when I swore it had a leak.

To the veterans, families, and medical staff at Bethesda Naval Hospital, thank you for reinforcing my belief that praying for peace and supporting our troops are not mutually exclusive acts.

Finally, my utter admiration goes out to the survivors of brain injuries and their families, both civilian and military. Thank you all for sharing your personal stories with me over the past two years on the road. Your journeys, struggles, and triumphs have made my own life brighter. I pray that no one else will ever have to walk in our shoes.

Photograph Credits

ABOUT THE AUTHOR

LEE WOODRUFF is the life and family contributor for ABC's *Good Morning America* and a freelance writer. She is on the board of trustees of the Bob Woodruff Family Foundation (Remind.org), a nonprofit organization that provides critical resources and support to our nation's injured service members, veterans, and their families—especially those affected by the signature hidden injuries of war: traumatic brain injury, post-traumatic stress disorder, and combat stress. Lee Woodruff lives in Westchester County, New York, with her husband, ABC News anchor Bob Woodruff, and their four children.

Visit her website at www.LeeWoodruff.com.